Speak Czech Badly!

But Speak It Today!

by
William G. Karneges

A Cafe Lover's Guide™
Published by LingoArts
San Francisco • Prague

🔊 Get the Audio! 🔊

Get the audio files for where the icons appear in the book by sending an e-mail to the e-mail address hidden in the book.

LingoArts
San Francisco, California
Cafe Lover's Guide
Prague, Czech Republic
www.lingoarts.com

Copyright © 2015 by William G. Karneges

All rights reserved

All rights for this book and associated audio/visual material, including rights of reproduction and transmission in any form or by any means whatsoever, are reserved.

Speak Czech Badly™ is a trademark of the Speak a Foreign Language Badly™ series.

Designed by Luciform Graphics
Manufactured in the United States of America

Cover photos: Left, Pexel, CCO, Pixabay
Right, StockSnap.io, CCO, Jan Vašek

10 9 8 7 6 5 4 3 2 1

Speak Czech Badly

ISBN -13: 978-0-9822243-1-1
ISBN -10: 0-9822243-1-1
BISAC: Language Arts & Disciplines / General

Table of Contents

Preface 7

Foreword 8

Introduction
Bad Czech: The Method Behind the Madness 9

Section I

Czech Pronunciation 19

Subject pronouns Using the verb *to Be* 27

Using other Verbs: Get your motor runnin'. 37

What about me: Using object pronouns 44

Using adjectives: "The big black dog is tired." 46

Making 'WH' questions: who, what, when, etc., 48

Making requests with Could and Would 51

Pointing things out: This/That/these/Those 55

Establishing Existence: There is/there are 56

"I am hot." : Differences in using "I'm" 57

"Meet me at the Blue Cafe." : Prepositions Part 1 58

Cardinal Numbers 60

"Another beer, please": numbers and quantifiers	62
Telling clock and calendar time Part 1	63
Ordinal Numbers	67
Expressing likes and dislikes	69
No, if's and's or but's: connecting words	70
Prepositions of location/directions/relationships	72
Me, **Myself** and I: using *se* part 1	75

Section II

The Czech Language Brain   77

Section III

Gold Medal Czech   127

Nouns are sexy in Czech: Using cases	128
No, a, the, or an: This and That revisited	151
Me again: 6 ways to say You or Me	156
My stuff: Almost 36 ways to say My	159
Adjectives: In Living Color	163
How to Create a Verb Brain	169

Nobody's Perfect or Imperfect verb use	174
What's done is done: Past tense	177
Word order: John bananas likes: wrong	179
More Future Imperfect	182
Call Me! The Imperative	184
Adverb use	187
What's the date today Part 2	190
Shoulda, woulda, coulda: Modal Verbs	192
Why are you doing that? Using Aby	199
Telling time Part 2	201
They have a daughter **who** lives in Spain	203
Who and What change form!	204
Which/What kind of change form!	205
Numbers change form, too.	207
Reflexive: Si and Se revisited	214
Passive aggressive	215
Terms of Endearment	217
Appendix	218
Demonstrative Adjectives	218

Czech Prefixes and Suffixes   220

Verb Classes   221

Verbs Expanded   224

Dictionary   239

Preface

As an English teacher of students in countries where English is a foreign language, I have spent countless hours in classes, cafes, pubs and shops trying to communicate with people who do not speak English, or who do not speak it very well.

Of the second group, the one thing I kept saying to myself was that I would be thrilled to speak their language at least as well as they are speaking mine. So in the process of realizing this goal, I have developed a shortcut which greatly facilitates conversation between people who do not speak each other's language.

I have created what I call "The Language Brain." It's a sort of cheat sheet which I bring with me to help me say what I want to the people I encounter in the countries I am visiting and working in. It gets me speaking the language right away which provides the practice necessary to really learn the language.

It was also inspired by the times I have spent with others, and that I have seen others spend, with only a bilingual dictionary in a café trying to make sense to one another. This is, I believe, a major improvement on that theme.

Unlike a phrase book which allows you to say only what is included there, and unlike a language course which takes far too long for most people's purposes, The Language Brain enables you to create novel statements, questions and sentences. And yes, like it says on the cover, in minutes. (That is, after you make it through my lengthy explanations. :-)

There are few experiences in life more enriching than having a dialogue, however short, in a foreign language. I once met a man who speaks several languages, and he said that for every language you speak you gain a new life. What a beautiful thought. I now agree and I hope you too discover a new life after using The Language Brain to help you have your first encounter in the Czech language.

Bon Voyage. Oops that's French, but we use it in English too, so it's ok. (The Czechs say, "Šťastnou cestu!", which you will learn how to pronounce shortly.)

Foreword

A Rich Foreign Language Experience

If you've ever attempted to learn a foreign language, you know what a difficult and frustrating experience it can be. You may start out with high hopes and enthusiasm, yet in a short time you give up, believing you have no aptitude for learning a foreign language and without the ability to even order a cup of coffee in the language you were learning.

This sad state of affairs is caused, I think, by traditional language learning methods which focus on grammatical precision and the memorization of words. This approach is necessarily time-consuming and confusing which leads to a high failure rate.

If we start our language studies with the intention of learning a language in real-time and with few errors, we will fall into the trap of learning little and most likely quit in a short time.

But if we use the guided approach offered here, or what I call "Paper Conversation," we can learn to create a lot of language in little time and have a ball while visiting the Czech Republic. Then, if you continue to speak in the new language, you will internalize the language, remember words without trying, and develop the ability to converse in real-time with fewer and fewer errors.

Ironically, this approach is the fastest way to speaking a language in real-time. Not surprisingly, because this is a learning by doing approach. As crazy as it may sound, we will not burden the learning process by placing demands on the memory portion of our brains.

There are too many beautiful languages and too little time to learn them all well. But now, with the help of the Language Brain, it is possible to have a rich foreign language experience in very little time, and speak many languages... badly! I believe this orientation will encourage more people to go further in more languages than anyone ever dreamed possible.

Introduction

Bad Czech
The Method Behind the Madness

The Language Brain

"The Language Brain" is based on the fact that there are two major groups of words in most all languages. The first group are called functional words, which include words like *and, if, also, with,* and others. In this category there are approximately 200 words. We use the words from this group very frequently to help us construct almost every sentence we say. In the second group are words like *house, run, pen, tree,* and all the others. In the English language, this group has approximately 1 million words. Although some of the words from this group are used frequently, like the word *food* for instance, others almost never, like the word *discombobulate*. As you can see, there is a vast difference in the number of words in each group and the frequency with which they are used, the importance of which will soon be illustrated.

To give you an idea of how these words work, consider the words *studies* and *Tom*. In English we can combine these two words in only one way to make a complete thought, and that is:

Tom studies.

Both of these words are from the second group. These words tell us a little something about who and what but nothing about where, or precisely when, why or how. If we want to provide answers to these questions, we need to add words from the functional group of words. Let's see what this does to our sentence.

Tom studies in the library with Susan, on Fridays at 3:00, so she will fall in love with him.

By adding the functional words, in, with, on, at, and so, we are able to say where, in the library, something about how, with Susan, when, on Fridays at 3:00, and why, so she will fall in love.

As you can see from this example, words from both groups are necessary to create meaningful and useful statements.

If we imagine communication as the movement of a car, and language the engine and fuel, then the words from the first group, the functional words, are the engine and the words from the second are the fuel.

You absolutely need a car with a complete engine, but you don't need much gasoline to start the engine and make the car move.

So, what we need when learning a new language is to build the language engine as quickly as possible so we can get behind the wheel and make the car move, that is, make some meaningful conversation, like, "I would like another beer, please."

Fortunately, it doesn't require very many words to build the language engine. If you remember, there are only two hundred functional or "language engine" words, and we use even less—about half that amount in daily conversation.

But what about the remaining one million words that will make our car go fast and far. There is good news here as well. Of those million words, most of us know about 30,000, and even better, only 3000 words account for over ninety percent of most written and spoken communication and out of those 3000 words, it only takes about a 1000 to express almost any thought you have. (And even fewer, for those of us who have fewer thoughts) Wow, I'm excited! Where do I sign up?

All the parts of the language engine to the Czech language are included in The Language Brain at no extra charge. I want to get you behind the wheel and get your car, or rather, your mouth, moving as quickly as possible. That's why they call me a motor mouth. (And just when you thought this metaphor was falling apart, it comes roaring back.) Varrooooom!

Language Hurdles

All languages have similar hurdles that need to be navigated when learning them. Four important ones include: pronunciation, memory, comprehension, and correctness.

1. Pronunciation: Your pronunciation doesn't need to be perfect, but it must be good enough to be understood by native Czech speakers. Speaking is a motor skill. So, learning a language is like learning a new sport. Your mind, breath, vocal chords, tongue, and lips will be trying to produce sounds they have never produced before. It takes practice to learn the movements to a new sport. That's why it is essential to say the words aloud as much as possible. Having an accent only makes you more attractive, so don't worry about it.

Also, what you hear and what is being said are often two different things, as your ears are unaccustomed to hearing these exotic sounds. Your listening ability will also improve with practice.

Using The Language Brain requires the ability to pronounce Czech words from their written form. So, we will be working on this skill right from the beginning of this course. (As a side benefit you will be learning how to read Czech)

2. Memory: Another unique feature to this approach is that you will not be asked to memorize anything. This overcomes a major language learning obstacle, to say the least. By not limiting ourselves to what we have memorized, we will be able to communicate a great deal in very little time with the paper conversation approach mentioned earlier. In a conventional language course, it may take months before you are even exposed to material that you can learn to put into use almost immediately with the visual aid of "The Language Brain".

Not only is this approach a very effective stepping stone to speaking the language in real-time, but it will also allow more people to have a rich foreign language experience that they would not otherwise have been able to have. In the context of sitting in a café or pub and trying to make conversation with a new friend from a foreign land, this approach is unbeatable.

There is no faster way to develop speaking abilities in a foreign language than through the guided approach offered by The Language Brain. You will automatically begin to remember the words as you use them to communicate your thoughts in a real context. The best way to learn something is to do it.

3. Comprehension: Unfortunately, though, extensive listening skills cannot be learned quickly. Not only is the sheer volume of possible things you might hear overwhelming, but you will be hearing it at real-time speed. This is not something that can be learned overnight. You can control what you say and the speed at which you say it, but not what you hear. However, by leading the conversation in a foreign language you can limit the possible responses you hear and reduce the load on your listening ability. That is the best tactic for managing what you hear.

4. Correctness: Another major obstacle to the immediate use of a foreign language is the demand to be grammatically perfect. As a beginner, you are entitled to make a lot of mistakes. As long as key elements of the language are correct, it is possible to make errors in other areas and still be understood. Allowing ourselves this freedom will enable us to comprehensibly communicate a great deal very quickly. Language is complex and can be overwhelming if you try to do everything perfectly from the start.

You only need to be correct enough to be understood. However, this course gives you the option of choosing which level of correctness you want to use. In "Gold Medal Czech" Section III, you can learn "perfect" Czech grammar, but in the beginning, the more correct you want to be, the longer it will take for you to say what you want to say. What do levels of correctness mean? Look at the following sentences and an imaginary Olympic rating of them:

Levels of correctness   Olympic Rating

1. I am going to a restaurant with Tom.—Very good! 10 points

2. I go restaurant with Tom.— OK--I understand 5 points

3. Me go restaurant and Tom—Not Bad- I still understand 3.8 points

4. Restaurant Tom is I.—Very Bad--I'm not clear on this. 2 points-last place

Notice how all, except the last sentence, get the idea across that the speaker is going to a restaurant. Not a bad start.

The Goal of Speak Czech Badly

In this course, you will learn to create Gold Medal Czech. However, in the beginning, that is not our goal.

Our goals are at once more humble *and* more ambitious. While avoiding the very bad level four, we will be shooting for the ability to create hundreds of novel and useful statements somewhere between levels one and three.

Will you say everything correctly? Most definitely not. And neither does anyone else even after years of study. But you will say more than most people ever say in a foreign language—and that's saying something!

The Grammar Dilemma

Most of us have forgotten whatever grammar terms we may have learned. As a result, I have found that using grammar terms to teach grammar, often hinders more than it helps the understanding of grammar.

And of course we all learned our first language without consciously learning any grammar rules or terms at all. Linguists are still trying to unravel the rules we use to speak by.

However, when learning a new language, we will, in the beginning, have to make conscious the learning of grammar operations. The theory behind learning grammar is that once a rule is learned you will be able to apply the rule to each new word you encounter. So rather than memorize all the forms a word takes, you would simply apply the rule. At first, this operation is conscious, slow and plodding. But with practice this operation becomes automatic as it takes place at the subconscious level.

For example: If you had to learn the imaginary English verb curple, you would automatically know that he curpled yesterday and that I curple but that he and she curples. This automatic process takes place at the subconscious level in the language engine that was built when you were a child. Of course, there are exceptions, but that's the general idea.

The subconscious learns that this is what it is supposed to do with words like that. So, what are the words like that?

Language Fuel Words

1. **Nouns**: dogs and cats, Jack and Jill, Paris and pantyhose, sex and drugs and rock and roll are all nouns. Nouns name people, places, things, ideas, or qualities.

2. **Adjectives**: describe nouns as in, Jack is short, or Give me a big bag, or green bag, or words like gentle, small, and tired. Also included here are numbers and quantifiers such as, one, two, three, all, a few, some, etc, and when we say this or that person or thing. Also, the articles *a, an* and *the* can be included here.

3. **Verbs**: express various types of actions like, sleeping, eating, becoming, and also states like to know and to understand. I know him.

4. **Adverbs**: mostly describe verbs as in, Jack ran *quickly* up the hill.

Language Engine Words

5. **Pronouns**: usually substitute for nouns, as in, Jack likes her (her meaning Jill). She likes him. Her, she, him, along with we, they, this, that, their, my and several other words are pronouns. (The personal pronouns, he, him, his, her, etc. are the words spoken most often, so these are the words we need to become most familiar with when learning a new language.)

6. **Prepositions**: show the location and relationship between things as in, Jack and Jill went *up* the hill. *Up, down, in, at, on to, with, for about*, and *of* are prepositions.

7. **Conjunctions**: are connecting words like Jack *and* Jill. Words like *and, also, but, because, if, however, whenever,* and others are conjunctions.

Any thought you have which finds its way out of your mouth contains more or less information. From a simple "Wow", to "Four score and seven years ago…". Additionally, most sentences have at minimum an actor, or subject, like Bob , for instance, and an action or verb, like, eats. Sentences can be expanded to include an object for the verb, such as, bananas, and may include one or more circumstances surrounding this event such as a time, place, reason or murder weapon.

"Bob eats bananas at home in the morning with a spoon."

Can you identify all the parts of speech in the preceding sentence?

How Language is Created

Language is created with the parts of speech. That is, we mostly talk about people, places and things (pronouns and nouns), which are doing something (verbs) at a particular place or time (expressed with the help of prepositions). If we want to qualify or quantify a person, place or thing or say how something is done, we use adjectives and adverbs. Then, if we don't want anybody else to get a word in edgewise, we keep talking with the help of conjunctions.

Fortunately, people, places and times come from a limited set of words and expressions. For example, me, myself and I (my and mine) are the only ways I can refer to myself in English. Although Czech has considerably more pronoun words, they too come from a limited set.

Places and times too come from an almost limited set of expressions. You are usually at home, work, school, in the car, in a store, in the kitchen, bathroom or bedroom.

Of course, there are other places in the city and country or mountains and seaside but these are mostly from a fairly common and small set of words.

Time expressions include phrases like the day after tomorrow, in the morning, at night and other common and limited sets of expressions

Although there are thousands of verbs, we use a surprisingly small number with great frequency in everyday conversation.

In contrast, things (nouns) come from an almost endless supply of words, too many for anyone in any language to know them all. But as mentioned earlier, we use only a small portion of these words for most of our communication needs. The word list in the Language Brain Section and the all-purpose and high frequency words included in the vocabulary list will allow you to speak about a wide variety of topics.

The Language Brain Section beginning on page 77 contains most of these limited sets of time and space expressions, people and thing quantifiers and qualifiers and other key words.

In Section I, you will learn the following simple sentence patterns that will allow you to literally plug in these expressions, which will enable you to comprehensibly communicate a great deal very quickly.

You will learn to make these statements negative, as in, John wasn't in the library, and questions--Does he like bananas? And to do this all in the past, present and future.

To Be Verbs

John	is	eating
	was	a student
	will be	hungry
		in the library

These simple patterns along with other tenses and functions are the pistons to our language engine. They form the basis for almost everything we say. In Section III you will learn to qualify these statements to express more complex thoughts.

This Book

This book is divided into four sections. The first section teaches pronunciation and shows you how to form statements and questions, both positive and negative. In this section, you will get lots of practice in "The Language Creation Labs." This section focuses on the basic sentence patterns we use in everyday speech to express most of the thoughts we have.

The second section is where The Language Brain is located. Here you will put to use what you learned to do in Section I. You will use this section when you are sitting in a café in Prague and want to make instant conversation in the Czech language. The Language

Brain has the most useful compilation of handy charts containing the language engine words and phrases. By having these key words available at your fingertips, you will instantly be able to say almost anything you want.

The third section takes us under the hood and explores the inner workings of Czech grammar. It is ready, when you are ready, to take your Czech to the next level. It also contains a few more sentence patterns that require more grammar knowledge to put into use. Enter this section at your own risk because Czech grammar may be hazardous to your mental health.

The fourth section is an alphabetical vocabulary list of the key words we use in daily conversation. They cover broad topic areas thereby allowing you to comment on a variety of subjects. Additionally, the words are labelled to allow easy grammatical manipulation of them.

If you purchased the print, Kindle or ePub version of this book you can access the audio icons by sending an e-mail to paxbk@hotmail.com. The link or files will be sent to you. At present, only the print version is available.

Section 1: Czech Pronunciation

Can you say "Strč prst skrz krk"?

First the bad news

There are two sounds in the Czech language that are particularly difficult to learn to pronounce properly. These sounds both involve the pronunciation of the letter r. Czech has two r's and one of them is especially difficult to pronounce. In fact, it is listed in the Guinness Book of World Records as the most difficult sound to pronounce. Well, it should be, if it isn't. :-)

R's seem to be a problem in most languages. It seems that every language has its own peculiar way of pronouncing this letter which gives everyone else in the world a problem. Mispronouncing difficult sounds is half the fun and forms the basis of many endearing friendships. That said, let's not begin here but begin at the beginning and deal with the r's in turn.

And now the good news

The good news is that written Czech is phonetic, which means that the words are pronounced as they are spelled. Once you learn how the letters are pronounced, you will be able to pronounce most words properly. Also, all the letters are pronounced in Czech words. Not so in English. Although we do pronounce all the letters to the word dog, try explaining the missing w sound in the word two and why it appears in the word one.) This is why learning to read English gives everyone else in the world a big headache.

The other good news is that most all words in the Czech language are pronounced with the stress on the first syllable. Consider the words present and present. Without context you don't know how to pronounce these words.

present—(as in a gift) the stress is on the first syllable

present—(as in a presentation) the stress is on the second syllable

Do realize that the pronunciation of single alphabet letters and the way these letters are pronounced in words are not always identical. This is particularly true in English. Consider the letter c, pronounced like an *s* as in the word *see*. Yet, it is pronounced like k in the word cat. Although Czech letters tend to more closely represent their pronunciation in words, there are occasional variants.

About the Audio Icons

Send an e-mail to paxbk@hotmail.com., and a link or files will be sent to you so you can listen to and practice the pronunciation of the Czech letters and all the other language associated with the audio icons in this book.

Czech uses diacritical marks above letters to indicate changes in pronunciation of various letters. The two most common are the little *v* symbol called the háček or little hook in Czech and the slanted line accent mark called the čárka. The sounds they make are explained in the descriptions of the letters below.

The Czech Alphabet

(Repeat after speaker, pause recording if necessary)

    a ah like the a in auto
    á aah this accent mark means to hold the letter about twice as long, (all the vowels are made long with this accent mark)
    b like the English b
    c like the last two letters in bats or chance
    *ch like the ch in loch ness monster
    č like the ch in church
    d like the English d
    d' combine the letter d with the y sound in yellow {dya}

e like the e in bet
é long e vowel, almost pronounced like the ai in bait
ě like the y sound in yellow {yeh} or yet
f like the English f
g like the g in grace
h like the h in heart (the h is always said strongly)
i like the i in bit or like beet said quickly
í held longer, like eee
j like the y in yes
k like the English k
l like the English l
m like the English m
n like the English n
ň like the n in canyon
o like the o in mow
o´ long o, like th o in goal
p like the English p but shorter and a bit softer
q kveh-seldom occurs in traditional Czech words
r rolled like the Scottish r
ř a sound unique to Czech-combine r and ž (below)
s like the English s
š like the s in shore
t like the English t
ť combine a soft t with the y in yellow
u like the oo sound in moon but shorter
ú long u, like the oo in moon, (used at the beginning of words)
ů like ú but used in the middle and end of words
v like the English v
w like v (found only in borrowed foreign words)
x iks (found in borrowed foreign words)
y like the English ee sound (same as the Czech i)
ý long y sound like eee
z like the English z
ž like the s in treasure and pleasure

*(The ch letter combination usually appears after the letter h in Czech dictionaries.)

Pronunciation Rules

Rule 1. Letter combinations

At any opportunity, the Czech language seems to want to create the yeh sound as in yet. We have already heard it with d', ě , j, and t'. Here are some letter combinations that also produce this sound.

dě sounds like dyeh	děkuji (thank-you)
ně sounds like nyeh	někde (somewhere)
tě sounds like tyeh	ještě (still)
bě sounds like byeh	běhat (to run)
pě sounds like pyeh	pětka (the number five)
vě sounds like vyeh	věk (age)
mě mnyeh	mě (me)

(This one is unique because it is pronounced as if there were an *n* between the *m* and *ě*, as if it should be written as mně) in fact these two words exist in Czech and they are pronounced the same.

Rule 2. These letter combinations create a softening effect almost wherever they appear:

di dyee divadlo

ni nyee sloni (elephants)

ti tyee děti (children)

(This effect does not occur with long í combinations as in dí, ní, tí.)

Rule 3. Diphthongs are letter combinations that produce new sounds. There are only three in Czech.

ou is pronounced like "oh"- novou (new)

au is pronounced like "ow"- auto (auto)

eu (both letters are pronounced, sort of like, eh/ew

Rule 4. The pronunciation of the letters in the first column change to the pronunciation of the letters in the second column when:

A. they appear at the ends of words

b—p	dub (bread) sounds like *dup*
v—f	Václav sounds like *Váhclaf*
d—t	led sounds like *let*
ď—ť	loď sounds like *loť*
z—s	ztratit sounds like *stratit*
ž—š	tužka sounds like *tuška*
h—ch	vrah sounds like *vrach*

B. and when they appear before any of the letters in the second column.

obchod   (the *b* precedes *ch* is pronounced like p and the d is pronounced like t)

g—k   Oleg (Olek)

Rule 4a. And conversely, the letters in the second column are pronounced like the letters in the first column when they come before the letters in the first column. This mostly involves the letter k becoming a g sound as in :

kde pronounced gde (soft g sound as in get)

Pronunciation Lab

Practice saying these words

Practice 1. Place stress on first syllable

pane (Mr., when calling out to a man)

narození (birth)

nemocnice (hospital)

Practice 2. Pronounce all the letters (remember to pronounce the last e as well)

policie (police)

ulice (street)

zelenina (vegetables)

restaurace (restaurant)

Practice 3. Hold the long vowels about twice as long. (compare)

tanec-táta (dance-daddy)

pes-léto (dog-summer)

pivo-blízko (beer-near)

loterie-citrón (lottery-lemon)

ulice-únor (street-February)

(remember, ů is also a long u)

student-sůl (student-salt)

(also ý is long)
tady-nový (here-new)

Practice 4. Change the pronunciation of these words according to rule number four:

Kdy pronounced (gdy)   (when)

Kdo pronounced (gdo)   (who)

Kde pronounced (gde)   (where)

Practice 5. Pronounce these dipthongs

koule   (ball)

zeus   (greek god)

Practice 6. Letter combinations-di, ni, ti

lodě   (ships)

divadlo   (theater)

tikat   (tick)

Practice 7. Letter combinations- with ě

mně   (me)

město   (city)

tělo   (body)

pět   (five)

Practice 8. Some prepositions are not pronounced separately but become the beginning of the following word in the sentence.

v knihovně (in the library) is pronounced (fknihovně)

k obědu   (for lunch)

s tebou   (with you)

Practice 9. The j sound is often lost in colloquial speech when it begins words as in;

jsi   (you)

jste   (you, plural/formal)

Read these sentences aloud then listen to the audio.

1. The boy is over there. = Ten kluk je tamhle.

2. That man speaks English. = Tamten muž mluví anglicky.

3. She is my sister. = Ona je moje sestra.

*Final note: The punctuation for signifying a soft letter t and d may appear as d' and t' or as Ď and Ť.

Subject Pronouns

How to make positive statements
How to make negative statements
How to ask questions with the verb *to be*

How to make positive statements

The first major difference between Czech and English is that where we take three words to say something like:

I am waiting. Czechs can say it with one word: čekám

The Czech word for I is já.
The Czech word for I am is jsem. *
The Czech word for wait is čekat.
But the Czech word for I am waiting or I wait is čekám. (all the ideas can be combined into one word)

já and *jsem* are often used in statements like:

I am a teacher = Já jsem učitel*. Or you could simply say—jsem učitel, because jsem can mean *I am*. (já is used for emphasis otherwise jsem can be used alone) (Czech doesn't use articles: a, an or the) Or I am tired. = Jsem unavený.

Czech words often show the difference between male and female counterparts. So, if you were a female, you would say: I am a teacher = Já jsem učitelka, instead of učitel or I am tired = Já jsem unavená—notice how the endings to the word teacher and tired changes to the letter *a, or ka* which is a common ending for feminine words.

Or I am in the library = Já jsem v knihovně.

The first example shows what you are doing. (a verb) I am waiting.
The second, what you are (a noun). I am a teacher.
The third, how you feel (an adjective). I am tired.
The fourth, where you are (a place). I am in the library.

*Note: jsem is also used in the past tense as you will soon learn.

How to make negative statements

Negation is very easy in Czech. You simply add the letters *ne* before the verb. So, I am = jsem and I'm not = nejsem. The exceptions are with he, she and it. For example: He is = (On) je and He isn't = není or (On není) A "No" People Brain chart appears in a few pages for clarity if needed.

How to make positive and negative questions

Question making with the verb *to be* is even easier! In English, we can sometimes ask questions simply with a rising intonation as in: "You want to talk to me." We often do this to verify what we heard or we say it in disbelief, but it's a question nonetheless.

Czech uses this rising intonation technique to make yes/no type questions out of most statements.

You are a teacher. = Jste učitel.   Are you a teacher? = Jste učitel?

Same words, same order but you simply rise, not raise your voice, at the end of the sentence otherwise it will be mistaken for a statement and not a question. Listen to the difference in the audio clip. Negative questions are simply negative statements with rising intonation.

We can already say a great deal once we plug in the different places to go and people to see. We usually talk about each other, so let's start there.

Look at the People Brain chart below. By finding the person you want to talk about (I, you, he, she, we, Bob, etc.) and the time (past, present or future), and the words we know, teacher, tired, in the library, and knowing how to form the negative and questions, "The People Brain" will allow you to create several novel sentences.

On the next page there are sentences for you to translate and then say. Get a pen and a piece of paper to write your answers on.

Ok! Let's make some language! (I said in minutes, didn't I)

Translate the sentences on the next page using The Czech People Brain below.

The Past, Present and Future of all persons in one handy chart.

The Czech People Brain

I = Já
Present—I am—(já) jsem
Past—I was—If you are a man you would say byl jsem
If you are a woman you would say byla jsem
Future—I will be—(já) budu

You = Ty
Present—You are—(ty) jsi
Past—You were—when addressing
a man you would say byl jsi
when addressing a woman you would say byla jsi
Future—You will be—(ty) budeš

He = On
Present—He is—(on) je
Past—He was—byl
Future—He will be—bude

She = Ona
Present—she is—(ona) je
Past—she was—byla
Future—she will be—(ona) bude

Bob = Bob
Bob is—Bob je
Bob was—Bob byl
Bob will be—Bob bude

We = My
Present—We are—(my) jsme
Past—We were—byli jsme
Future—We will be—budeme

You/formal/plural = Vy
Present—You are—(vy) jste
Past—You were—byli jste
Future—You will be—(vy) budete

They = Oni
Present—They are—(oni) jsou
Past—They were—byli
Future—They will be-(oni) budou

It = Ono/to
Present—it is—(ono) je
Past—it was—bylo
Future—it will be—(to) bude

SPEAK CZECH BADLY! BUT SPEAK IT TODAY!

Create Language Now!

Translate the sentences below using the sentence patterns and vocabulary in the chart below and The Czech People Brain on the previous page.

1. You were tired =
2. He will be in the library =
3. Is she a teacher? =
4. They weren't in the library =
5. We are tired =

(Answers on page 32)

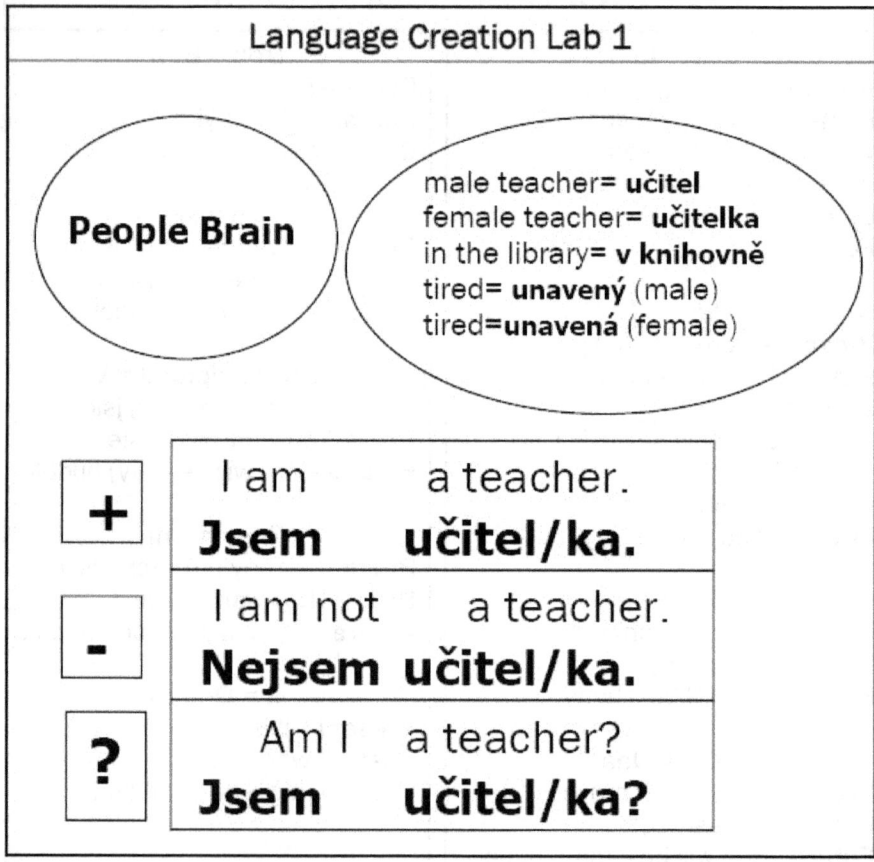

*Later we will learn other ways that Czech forms the future and how to make questions with the "WH" questions, ie., who, what , when, where,etc.

Language Power!

With just the three words, teacher, library and tired, it is possible to construct 252 novel statements with the seven subject pronouns in the past present and future and with positive and negative statements and questions. In fact, you should construct all these sentences on your own. It's the best drill for developing language fluency. Use the word Bob as a subject pronoun now and then too for practice.

The People Brain forms the core of our language engine. Let's consider for a moment the language power the People Brain offers.

All that we can say is, in a sense, an answer to one of the six basic questions—Who, What, When, Where, Why and How.

Now we can say who we are talking about—I, you, he, they, etc., and let's not forget 'it' which is included in the People Brain, which means we can begin to discuss just about anything.

We can say where we are—well, we can say we are in the library— but it's just a simple matter to substitute any other place. 'When' fits into the same slot as where, so as soon as we learn a when phrase, we can just tack it on.

And we can say all of these things in the past, present and future.

Shortly, we will learn how to say what we are doing in the library or anywhere else. And when we learn the word for 'because' we will be able to say why.

I don't know about you, but I'm getting excited because we are not that far off from being able to say almost anything we want. And it all starts with the People Brain!

Male and Female Differences

We learned that there are two words for *teacher* in Czech, one to show that the teacher is female and one to show that the teacher is male. If you were a female, you would use the female form when saying that you are a teacher. When talking to or about someone, you need to use the appropriate form. If you are talking about a female teacher you would say, "She is a teacher." = (Ona) je učitelka, which used the *ka* ending, as opposed to "He is a teacher." = On je učitel.

Czech makes this distinction when talking about occupations, nationalities, as in I am American = jsem Američan or if you are a female, "Jsem Američanka", and with some states of being like, *tired*, in the past tense and a few other situations which will be covered in detail in section three. For now just follow the charts and use the words provided in the language labs.

We are already able to communicate a great deal but we can't yet say, "They are teachers" because we don't know the plural for učitel and we can't say, "I was waiting," or "She waited," because we haven't learned how to use the verb čekat with different people or in different times (tenses).

Instructions for creating the plural can be found in Section III Shortly, we will practice making statements with wait and other verbs.

For now, let's learn the plural for teachers, which is učitelé, so we can use it in the next exercise.

     Answers to Lab #1

1) You were tired = Byl jsi unavený.

2) He will be in the library = Bude v knihovně.

3) Is she a teacher = Ona je učitelka?

4) They weren't in the library = Nebyli v knihovně.

5) We are tired = Jsme unavení.

Plug-in these words and translate the sentences below.

at work = v práci
at/in the restaurant = v restauraci
from California = z Kalifornie
teachers = učitelé
student = student (male)
student = studentka (female)
students = studenti
book = kniha
green = zelený
at 3 o'clock = ve tři hodiny
American (male) = Američan
British (male) = Angličan
Czech (female) = Češka

Language Creation Lab #2

11) The teachers are in the library =
12) Bob will be at work at 3 o'clock=
13) I'm from California=
14) The book is in the library=
15) The students were in the library=
16) The book is green=
17) We will be at the restaurant at 3 o'clock=
18) The student is tired=
19) He is American=
20) She is from California =

(Answers to Lab # 2 on page 34)

Answers for Language Creation Lab #2

11) The teachers are in the library =
Učitelé jsou v knihovně.

12) Bob will be at work at 3 o'clock=
Bob bude v práci ve tři hodiny.

13) I'm from California=
Jsem z Kalifornie.

14) The book is in the library=
Kniha je v knihovně.

15) The students were in the library=
Studenti byli v knihovně.

16) The book is green=
Kniha je zelená.

17) We will be at the restaurant at 3 o'clock=
Budeme v restauraci ve tři.

18) The student is tired=
Student je unavený.

19) He is American= On je Američan.

20) She is from California = Ona je z Kalifornie.

Are vs They are

Jsou can mean *they are-oni jsou* or just *are*. As in Jsou učitelé, meaning *They are teachers*, compared to, *The teachers are in the library*, which is Učitelé jsou v knihovně.

To Já or not to Já

Look back at the People Brain for a moment. Notice that *he* is, *she* is and *it* is, can all be expressed by the word *je*. The subject pronouns, on, ona, ono will only be added if there is some confusion as to who is being spoken about or for emphasis. In the same way, já and all of the other subject pronouns can be omitted because the verb incorporates the subject. In the case of *je*, it is the context which would show who or what was being spoken about.

A typical scenario would be if you were introduced to someone in an office, for instance. You might start by saying , I am John Smith-Já jsem John Smith. If you were then asked by the receptionist if you were American, you could answer with just "Ano, jsem Američan," without já. Which means, "Yes, I am American."

Familiar vs Formalities

Many languages, of which Czech is one, use a formal address when speaking to strangers, and people you don't know well enough to use the familiar address. This is accomplished by using the plural form of You. In the People Brain we saw the formal/plural form for you. So, when you want to say something like "How are you?", there are two variations depending on the you, you are speaking to.

How are you? =

Jak se máš? familiar
Jak se máte? formal

How are you guys? = Jak se máte?

There is a formal and informal variation for all verbs. We will practice these differences later, so you don't offend a shopkeeper when you ask if they have your favorite mineral water.

Just say No!
(How to make negative statements in Czech)

We can say "I am a teacher" so how do we say "I am not a teacher?" Saying no or not in Czech couldn't be simpler.

The word for no in Czech is ne. When this word is added to the beginning of verbs it negates them. For instance:

"I am a teacher." = Já jsem učitel.

"I am not a teacher." = Já nejsem učitel. (it's that easy)

The "No" Brain
with the verb to Be

I'm not = (já) nejsem
I wasn't = nebyl(a) jsem
I won't be = nebudu

You're not = (ty) nejsi
You weren't = nebyl(a) jsi
You won't be =   nebudeš

He isn't = (on) není
He wasn't = nebyl
He won't = nebude

She isn't = (ona) není
She wasn't = nebyla
She won't = nebude

It isn't = (ono) není
It wasn't = nebylo
It won't be = nebude

We aren't = (my)nejsme
We weren't = nebyli jsme
We won't be = nebudeme

You aren't = (vy) nejste
You weren't =nebyli jste
You won't be =nebudete

They aren't = nejsou
They weren't = nebyli
They won't be = nebudou

Bob isn't = Bob není
Bob wasn't = Bob nebyl
Bob won't be = Bob nebude

Get Your Motor Mouth Runnin' with other Verbs

So far, we have practiced only with the verb *to be*, i.e., am, are, is, was, etc.. But in order to express all the other actions and states such as, eating and working, to know and to understand, etc., we need other verbs.

Other verbs are the octane in our fuel mixture. They really get our communication vehicle moving. With the help of the Verb Brain on the next page we can exponentially expand what we can say. Take a moment and read the entire chart so you can see what you can say with it.

The first thing to note is that the person and verb are combined into one word, as mentioned earlier.
Thus, I am waiting = čekám.

Now look at the very first row in the verb brain. Notice that Czech has only one word to represent all of the tense aspects English has here for the word *wait*.

I wait—I am waiting—I have been waiting, are all expressed by the word čekám. The statements in all the other rows are also expressed with only one word
For instance:

He is waiting. = čeká
He has been waiting for 10 minutes. = čeká 10 minut.
He has been waiting since three o'clock. = čeká od tří hodin.
He waits every morning. = čeká každé ráno.

Notice that only the word čeká is used in all of these sentences! This will take a little getting used to as you will search for more variations where there are none.

Also notice, that only in the past tense are male and female differences shown in the verb. Thus, for example, "you waited," will be alternately, čekal jsi or čekala jsi (female) depending on the sex of the person speaking or being addressed.

The negative is formed in the same way as before—by adding the ne prefix. Thus, čekám becomes nečekám to say I am not waiting.

Yes/no questions are also formed with the rising intonation technique. So to ask "Are you waiting?", find the present tense you are waiting form and use a rising intonation. Thus, "čekáš?"

Do, Does, and Did Don't exist in the Czech Language

When you want to ask something like, "Do you wait every morning?" you will again, simply use the word čekáš to form this question. See the comparison below:

Are you waiting? = Čekáš?
Do you wait every morning = Čekáš každé ráno?

Since the verb combines the person and the action together, the rising intonation technique is able to form the question without the helping word 'do' that English needs.

Another way in which verb use differs from English is when giving a command or instruction as in "wait for me." In Czech, the verb changes form to indicate this use, explained in detail in Section III.

Czech makes a distinction between actions that are seen as ongoing and actions that are viewed as completed or one-time events known as *the perfective*. A different verb is used to express this view. The final panel gives a brief description but we will not practice this verb form until Section III, where a detailed explanation is given.

In Section III, you will learn the rules for creating a brain like this for every verb you need. But for now, let's put this one to good use in the language creation lab.

wait   Verb Brain #1   čekat

I wait, I am waiting, I have been waiting,	= čekám
you wait, you are waiting, you have been waiting	= čekáš
he / she / it waits, is waiting, has been waiting	= čeká
we wait, we are waiting, we have been waiting	= čekáme
they wait, they are waiting, they have been waiting	= čekají
you wait (plural/formal) **Present**	= čekáte

I waited, I was waiting, I have waited,	= čekal jsem (male),
	= čekala jsem (female)
you waited, you were waiting,	= čekal jsi, čekala jsi
he	= čekal
she waited, was waiting, has waited,	= čekala
it	= čekalo
we waited, were waitng,	= čekali jsme
they waited, they were waiting,	= čekali
you (plural/formal) **Past**	= čekali jste

I	= budu čekat
you	= budeš čekat
he	
she ——— will wait	= bude čekat
it	
we	= budeme čekat
they	= budou čekat
you (plural/formal) **Future**	= budete čekat

Wait! (The Imperative)

In English, we use the word *wait*, whether we say I will wait or when we instruct someone to wait, as in "wait a minute." Czech uses a different form to show this distinction and it varies depending on who you are saying it to.

Wait for me said to one person : čekej

Wait for me said to two or more people: čekejte

Let's wait: čekejme

The Perfective

Although Czech does not use all the verb forms of English, it does use another verb idea known as the *perfective*. It is used to express a completed or one time activity in the past or in the future. The perfective form of *wait* in Czech is *počka*t. See Page 174 for *the perfective*.

Language Creation Lab # 3
(positive/negative statements/questions with other verbs)

Making Language is Easy!
Just plug-in the words you need from each bubble.

Verb Brain
see opposite page

15 minutes = 15 minut
every morning = každé ráno
since two o'clock = od dvou hodin

| I am waiting |
| **Čekám** |

Create Language Now!
Translate and say these statements.

1) He is waiting =
2) She has been waiting for 15 minutes =
3) Do you wait every morning?
4) Does she wait here?
5) They have been waiting since two o'clock.
6) We are waiting in the library.
7) He isn't waiting.
8) Is Bob waiting?
9) I will be waiting there.
10) Did she wait at home?

(Answers to Lab #3 on page 41)

Lab #3 Answers

1. He is waiting =
   (On) Čeká.

2. She has been waiting for 15 minutes =
   Čeká už 15 minut.

3. Do you wait every morning? =
   Čekáš každé ráno?

4. Does she wait here? =
   Čeká tady?

5. They have been waiting since two o'clock. =
   Čekají už od dvou hodin.

6. We are waiting in the library.=
   Čekáme v knihovně.

7. He isn't waiting.=
   On nečeká.

8. Is Bob waiting?=
   Čeká Bob?

9. I will be waiting there.=
   Budu tam čekat.

10. Did she wait at home? =
    Čekala doma?

The Top 20 Verbs

On the last few pages of Section II you will find a list of the verbs we use most in daily conversation. They are shown in their past, present and future forms. When you need to use one of these verbs, you will simply refer to that section. These verbs include:

have-mít	say-říkat or říct	can-moci or moct
go-jít	think-myslet	have to-muset
want-chtít	do-dělat	know-vidět
work-pracovat	need-potřebovat	come-přijít

For example: This is how the verb want appears on page 85 in The Language Brain Section.

Present
I want	chci	we want	chceme
you want	chceš	you want	chcete
he,she,it	chce	they want	chtějí

Past
I wanted	chtěl jsem	we wanted	chtěli jsme
you wanted	chtěl jsi	you wanted	chtěli jste
he wanted	chtěl	they wanted	chtěli
she wanted	chtěla		
it wanted	chtělo		

Future
I will want	budu chtít	we will want	budeme chtít
you will want	budeš chtít	you will want	budete chtít
he,she,it	bude chtít	they will want	budou chtít

By having these verbs ready to use, you can immediately put them to use and also start practicing with them in the following way.

Language "Shadow Boxing" Practice

Even before you consciously learn the rules for using verbs, you can begin to train your subconscious, because grammar usage at its best is ultimately a subconscious activity. You can do this in the same way boxers shadow box to practice their moves.

For instance, if you wanted to practice with the verb čekat, you would practice saying the following questions and answers: translated into Czech, of course.

Are you waiting? Čekáš?
Yes, I'm waiting. Ano, čekám.
Isn't she waiting? Ona nečeká?
No, she isn't waiting. Ne, nečeká.
Is he waiting? Čeká?

And so on. Your goal is to practice all of the combinations, in the past, present and future, in questions and statements in the affirmative and negative.

This will help you remember the words of course, but more importantly it will help train your subconscious to change the form of the word when speaking to or about other people

The Infinitive

Whether in Czech, or English, the dictionary form of the verb is called the infinitive. This form is the starting point for all the changes that you see in the Verb Brain on page 39. In Section II, you will learn the rules for creating all the forms that you see in the Verb brain from the infinitive or dictionary form for any verb you need.

The 20 verbs listed on the previous page are in their infinitive form. Remember, that in English we use the infinitive to say *I wait* but in Czech you don't say Já čekat, you say Já čekám or just čekám. The infinitive changes form. Of course in English, *have* changes to *has* to say *he has*. So, the verbs in English sometimes change form as well, but in different ways.

Sometimes the infinitive is used in sentences without any change to it at all. Look at the Verb Brain and notice that in the future, the infinitive of čekat, along with the future of *to be* (být) is used to say, I will wait, budu čekat, you will wait, budeš čekat, etc. Here, the infinitive form --čekat-- is used.

There are other times when the infinitive is used as well. In English, we use the infinitive after certain verbs like want, for instance. We say, "I want to eat." The verb *to eat* remains in the infinitive in both of these statements. Czech also uses the infinitive after certain verbs, like want and in other situations, which will be discussed further in Section III.

What about me?
*Using Object Pronouns

We can now say, "She is waiting," but we can't say, "She is waiting for me," because we don't yet have the words for me or him, her, etc. See Mini Me brain to below. We will simply use these as we would in English.

Mini Me Brain	
me	mě
you	tebe
him	ho
it	ho
her	jí
us	nás
them	jich
you (formal/plural)	vás (formal/plural)
*with me	se mnou
with you	s tebou

Language Creation Lab #4

for = na
(Czech has other words for *for, which you will learn later*)

Create Language Now!

Translate and say these statements

She is waiting for me. =
I am waiting for you. =
He is waiting *with me. =

(Answers to Lab #s 4-6 on page 47)

*When saying *with*, Czech changes the form of these pronouns. We will observe the changes of me and you. In Section III, you will see all forms.

Is that my pen?
*Using Possessive Pronouns

We also don't yet have the words for my, your, etc. See the Mini My Brain below. Again, we will use these as we would in English.

Mini My Brain

my = moje   your = tvoje
his = jeho   its = jeho
her = její   our = naše
their = jejich   your = vaše (plural)

Language Creation Lab #5

pen = pero, that = to, over there = tamhle

Create Language Now!
Translate and say these statements.

1) Is that my pen? =
2) That is your pen =
3) Her pen is over there =

"The **big black** dog is tired."

*For basic adjective use, we will simply use adjectives as we do in English.

Thus, for a statement like: "The big black dog is tired." We first need to look in a Czech/English dictionary or in the vocabulary list at the back of this book for the basic adjectives we need to translate. There, we would find:

big = velký, black = černý, tired = unavený, is = je, dog = pes

Our grammatically incorrect yet understandable statement in Instant Czech would then read: **"Velký černý pes je unavený."**

Big, Bigger, the Biggest

In English, adjectives can be compared, as in, this is bigger than that, or that is the biggest dog I have ever seen. The same is true in Czech. *For most adjectives, the comparative is formed as follows:

1. start with the basic adjective as in : nový (new)
2. remove the last letter, which leaves: nov
3. add ější to the end: novější

To create *the newest,* simply add the prefix nej after you have formed the comparative (novější) thus we get: nejnovější.

Language Creation Lab #6

Vocabulary - these = tyto, those = tamty, shoes = boty, are = jsou, than = než

say : "These shoes are newer than those."=

*The complete use of adjectives, including irregulars, in the Czech language is explained in Section III. Also, see Communication tricks, page 77.

Answers Lab #4

1. She is waiting for me. = (Ona) čeká na mě.

2. I am waiting for you. = Čekám na tebe.

3. He is waiting with me. = (On) čeká se mnou.

Answers Lab #5

1. Is that my pen? = Je to moje pero?

2. That is your pen = To je tvoje pero.

3. Her pen is over there = Její pero je tamhle.

Lab #6
These shoes are newer than those. =
Tyto boty jsou novější než tamty.

Who/What/When/Where/Why/How?
Forming Info Questions

Earlier we looked at how Czech makes yes/no questions, that is, questions that can be answered with a simple yes or no, as in, "Are you a student?" Now we will learn how to form questions with the other type of questions, those which require more information in the answer, such as, "What time is it?" or "Where is the National Museum?" These are formed with question words much the same way as we do in English.

See the boxes below which show the English info question words and their Czech equivalents. In addition, Czech actually has a few question words that don't exist in English.

Who=Kdo Who is that? Kdo je to?	**What=Co** What is that? Co je to?	**When=Kdy** When does it start? Kdy to začíná?
Where=Kde Where is the castle? Kde jsou Hradčany?	**Why=Proč** Why not? Proč ne?	**How=Jak** How old is it? Jak je to staré?
To Where=Kam Where are you going? Kam jdeš?		**From Where=Odkud** Where are you from? Odkud jste?
Which=*Který Which one is better? Který je lepší?		**How much/many=Kolik** How much is it? Kolik to stojí?
Whose = Čí Whose pen is this? Čí je to pero?		**What kind of=*Jaký** What kind of films do you like? Jaké filmy se ti líbí?

In Section III, we wll see other variations of what and who.

SPEAK CZECH BADLY! BUT SPEAK IT TODAY!

Remember: No, *do, does, or did*, in Czech.

In English, we often combine the use of do, does, and did with these types of question as in, "When *does* the film start?" As we learned before, Czech does not use these helping words.

When does it start? = Kdy to začíná? Literally, (When it starts?)

Language Example Lab #7
Practice saying these questions and answers

1. What is that? It is ...
Co je to? To je...

2. Who is that? It is…—
Kdo je to? To je…

3. What do you think?—
Co (si) myslíš?

4. Where is it?---
Kde to je?

5. Where is the post office?---
Kde je pošta?

6. Where are you from? I'm from…
Odkud jsi? Jsem z …Ameriky.

*7. Why are you depressed?---
Proč jsi depresivní?

49

8. Why are you in the library?---
Proč jsi v knihovně?

9. Whose book is this?---
Čí je to kniha?

10. Which pen do you want?---
Jaké pero chceš?

11. How long is the film?---
Jak dlouhý je ten film?

12. How long is the desk?---
Jak dlouhý je ten stůl?

13. How far is it to Paris?---
Jak daleko je to do Paříže?

14. How often does Tram 22 come?---
Jak často jezdí dvacet dvojka?

15. How many hours do you sleep?---
Kolik hodin spíš?

16. How much is the pizza?---
Kolik stojí pizza?

17. How old are you?---
Kolik ti je?

18. How cold is it ?---
Jak studené je to?

In Section II, you will learn more common expressions and phrases.)

   * In Czech and some other European languages, the word sad/ smutný is more commonly used instead of the word depressed, which is used for the more severe type of clinical

SPEAK CZECH BADLY! BUT SPEAK IT TODAY!

"Prosím"

While travelling in the Czech Republic you will hear this all-purpose word frequently. It has several meanings. It can mean, please, you're welcome, if you please, pardon, and more. It is commonly used in the following situations:

1. Thank you in Czech is *Děkuju, you could reply with-Prosím (you're welcome)
2. When addressing someone to ask for assistance, as in, Excuse me, Where's the National Theater? Prosím vás, kde je Národní Divadlo?
3. To allow someone the right of way into an elevator or doorway, you can simply say: Prosím
4. Someone asks to use a chair at your table or for permission to do something, you say: Prosím
5. To get the attention of a waitress in a restaurant and immediately order something: Prosím, pivo. or Pivo, prosím.

*Thank you:
formal - Děkuji
informal - Děkuju
short informal - Díky

Making Offers/Invitations/Requests/ and asking for Permission or Possibility

All languages have polite ways of asking for help or permission, for ordering, making offers, invitations and requests. The examples below contain the key words which create the patterns for making such questions in the Czech language. The practice labs will highlight these patterns so you can use them in a variety of situations.

SPEAK CZECH BADLY! BUT SPEAK IT TODAY!

(Requests)
Could you help me?" Mohl bys mi pomocí?
Can you help me? Můžeš mi pomocí?

(Permission or possibility)
Could I use the computer? Mohl bych použít počítač?
Can I use the computer? Můžu použít počítač?

(Offering)
"Would you like a glass of water?" Chtěl bys skleničku vody?
Dáš si vodu? (Give you water?)

(Invitations)
"Would you like to go for a drink tonight?"
Chtěla bys jít dnes večer na drink? (a male asking a female)
Chtěl bys jít dnes večer na drink? (a female asking a male)

(In Czech, they often say go for a glass instead of go for a drink.)

"Could you...?"
Mohl bys...?

Language Creation Lab # 8 (requests)

Mohl is the past of the infinitive for can, which is moct. When it combines with the helping conditional *you* word bys, it creates the polite, could you = mohl bys, idea in Czech.

close = zavřít   window = okno   salt = sůl   pass = podat

Translate these sentences:

1. Could you close the window, please?
2. Could you pass the salt?

(Answers to Lab # 8 on page 54)

Could I...?
Mohl bych...? (permission, possibility)

Examples with Mohl

When *Mohl* combines with the helping conditional *bych*, it creates the *could I* idea in Czech.

Could I go on a internet? = Mohl bych jít na internet?
Could I go on a internet? = Mohl bych jít na internet?
Could + Infinitive

"Would you like to go for a drink sometime?"
Chtěl bys jít... (Invitations)

Examples with Invitations

Chtěl is the past of want and when it combines with the helping conditional you word bys, creates the would you like, or rather, semi-literally, would you want idea. Chtěl becomes chtěla when asked by or to a women.

Would you like to play tennis? = Zahrál by sis tenis?

Would you like to go to the cinema? = Šel bys do kina?

Would you like to have dinner tonight? = Šel bys dnes večer na večeři?

Would you like to go for a drink sometime? = Chtěl bys jít někdy na drink?

SPEAK CZECH BADLY! BUT SPEAK IT TODAY!

> ## "Would you like water?"
> ## Dáš si vodu? (Offering)

Language Creation Lab #9

English uses the *would you like* pattern for invitations, as well as for offers, and although Czech can use this variation for offering food or drink, it more typically uses the verb give, as in, "Can I give you"... Dáš si... or the more formal *Dal by sis* and then whatever item you are offering.

tea = čaj
Translate this question

Would you like (some) tea? =

I would like...

And of course you need to be able to say, *I would like,* so you can buy, order or request something. As always, there is more than one way to say something in a language and levels of politeness. The most common way in Czech is to say Dám si ...or Já si dám...Another more formal way is to say "Já bych si dal...and the item you want"

Answers Lab #8

Could you close the window, please?=
Mohl bys zavřít okno, prosím?

Could you pass the salt?=
Mohl bys mi podat sůl?

Answers Lab #9
Would you like a cup of tea? =
Dal by sis čaj?

Also, in English we can say, Do you *want* some water? Czech also uses the verb want in casual situations. So, it is possible to make offers and invitations with want like this:

Do you want some water? --- Chceš vodu?
Do you want to go to the cinema? --- Chceš jít do kina?

Likewise, in casual situations, you could use the more casual *can* and say, "Can I go on the internet?" Můžu jít na internet?

How to order in a restaurant

In a restaurant: From a waitress or waiter, you will likely hear: "Máte vybráno?", which means, "Have you chosen?" The typical response is: Já si dám, which literally means, *I will give myself*...and then the item you want.

In a shop: In a shop, if you want to be very polite, you can say, I would like ---Chtěl bych..., and then the item. You can use more casual responses, such as, I need, or I want---Potřebuji...or Já chci.... and the item you want. Do you have...? Máte or Nemáte...?

Nemáte means "Don't you have...?", which is often used in Czech and unlike English, is considered polite in Czech.

"Could I get a fork please?" Mohl bych dostat vidličku, prosím?
"Can you give me a napkin, please?" Můžeš mi podat ubrousek, prosím?

This/That/These/Those
Pointing things out in Czech

When pointing things out in English, we might say, for example: this pen-- if it is near to us or--that pen-- if it is further from us. We may also use *this* and *that* to distinguish between items, as in, "No, not that one, this one", or vice versa. We use *these* and *those* in the same way when talking about items in plural, ie., these pens, those

Czech has a much more elaborate system for distinguishing and identifying things and it is explained in greater detail in Section III, but for now we will use four all-purpose pronouns that we can use much in the same way as we do in English.

this--tohle   that--to

these--tyhle   those—tamty

One way in which Czech demonstrative pronoun use differs from English is when asking "What is that?" In English we say, what is that, or what are those, if we're asking about plural items. Czech uses the same question whether the items are singular or plural. Thus:

What is that (or it)? = Co je to?
Answer: That (or it) is a pen = To je pero.
What are those? = Co je to? Answer: Those are pens = To jsou pera.*

The answer, however, will be in the plural, if you are asking about plural items. Thus, to jsou pera. The question, "Co je to?" can mean, What is that/this/these/those or What is it?

There is/There are
Establishing existence in Czech

In English, the word *there* can mean a place, as in, "I was there once," or it is used for saying that something is or is not present, as in, "There are three pieces of bread left." We could even say something like, "There is a pool there," when referring to a hotel's facilities. The first *there* means that a pool exists or is present and the second *there* says where.

Czech does not use the word *there* to establish existence. Czech very simply uses je and jsou (is and are), which we first encountered in the People Brain.

There is a metro in Prague. Metro je v Praze. (singular)
There are pubs in Prague. Hospody jsou v Praze. (plural)

Of course, there is usually more than one way to express a thought. So, you could also express these thoughts by using have/has and say "Prague has a metro."(Praha má metro)

In a similar way, English uses the word *it* to act as a surrogate subject in statements such as "It is raining.", or " It is hot". In these sentences, *It* isn't referring to anything in the way it does when you say something like "It is a chair", (in this sentence, it refers to the chair). Czech, along with many other languages, does not use a surrogate subject in some common expressions. Thus:

It is hot = Je horko.   "It is raining" is one word. = Prší.

In everyday conversation, your English need to say *there is* and *there are* will occur frequently. So let's look at a couple more examples.

1. There is a book on the table.= Kniha je na stole.

2. There are beautiful lakes there.= Jsou tam nádherná jezera.

"I'm hot."

We learned that Czech, like English, uses *I am* or jsem or já jsem to say the following:

I am a teacher	já jsem učitel.
I am tired	jsem unavený
I am in the library	jsem v knihovně

In English, we can also say I am doing something, as in "I am waiting", but remember, that in Czech you cannot say, "*Já jsem čekat*", correct is čekám.

In English we also use *I am* to say:

I am hungry
I am cold
or most any other state of being (adjective)

Although Czech does use Já jsem (I am) to express most of these ideas, there are a few situations where it uses different constructions. Here are the most common exceptions:

I am hungry   Mám hlad. (Literally, I have hunger)
I am thirsty Mám žízeň

I am cold   Je mi zima. or (mně je zima) (It is to me cold)
I am hot   Je mi horko. or (mně je horko) (To me it is hot)

I'm scared   Mám strach (I have fear)

Although, it is possible to say I am warm = Já jsem teplý, or já jsem zima, the meaning is quite different . The former statement is slang and you would be stating that you were gay and in the latter that you were winter. Sometimes you just can't translate from one language to another and hope to be understood correctly. :-)

Meet me at the Blue Cafe
(where and when prepositions)

Each language has its own way of using prepositions, words like, on, at, and in. Sometimes these words are used in Czech in the same way as we use them in English and at other times differently. So, they really need to be learned situation by situation. Let's look at the most common uses below. (The Language Brain, page 77, contains an extensive list of where and when phrases.)

Where English uses the preposition on, Czech would use na or v.

in = v   at = v or u

to = do   on = na

Examples with Czech Prepositions

Let's meet at the Blue Cafe = Sejdeme se v Modré kavárně

I am in the library. = Jsem v knihovně

I'm home. = Jsem doma.

I'm in a car. = Jsem v autě

at five o'clock = v pět hodin

on Tuesday = v úterý

I'm already on the bus. = Už jsem v autobuse.

The book is on the table = Kniha je na stole

I'm going to Prague.= Jedu do Prahy.

Meet me at Můstek Metro station. = Sejdeme se na Můstku.

Meet me at the restaurant at five o'clock.= Sejdeme se v restauraci v pět hodin.

Your keys are on the chair. =Tvoje klíče jsou na židli.

I'm going to the store. = Jdu do obchodu.

Does this bus go to Florenc station? = Jede tento autobus do stanice Florenc?

Cardinal Numbers

zero	nula		
one	jeden	eleven	jedenáct
two	dva	twelve	dvanáct
three	tři	thirteen	třináct
four	čtyři	fourteen	čtrnáct
five	pět	fifteen	patnáct
six	šest	sixteen	šestnáct
seven	sedm	seventeen	sedmnáct
eight	osm	eighteen	osmnáct
nine	devět	nineteen	devatenáct
ten	deset	twenty	dvacet

(Notice that the "teens" all end in "náct" and all except fourteen, fifteen, and nineteen, simply use the single digit number as a prefix)

twenty-one	dvacet jedna
twenty-two	dvacet dva
twenty-three etc.	dvacet tři

thirty	třicet
forty	čtyřicet
fifty	padesát
sixty	šedesát
seventy	sedmdesát
eighty	osmdesát
ninety	devadesát
one hundred	sto
one thousand	tisíc
two thousand	dva tisíce
one million	jeden milion
two million	dva miliony
one billion	jedna miliarda
two billion	dvě miliardy

(As in English, we can alternately say, one thousand one hundred or eleven hundred. Czech also can use this variant. As in, tisíc sto or jedenáct set)

SPEAK CZECH BADLY! BUT SPEAK IT TODAY!

Beer, three times, please!

When you want to order two or three beers in a bar, here's how it's done.

When the waiter or waitress arrives and asks you what you would like, you would simply say:

one beer, please = "jedno pivo, prosím."

two beers, please = pivo, dvakrát, prosím

three beers, please = pivo, třikrát, prosím

Notice the word krát, it means times, as in multiply. So when you say dvakrát you are really saying beer, two times.

This is a common method used for buying or ordering more than one item of the same thing. So, when shopping for anything in any store, if you want two or more of the same item, you should use the word krát. (It is possible, however, to say two beers, please - dvě piva, prosím. By saying the item after the quantity you can avoid krát. But then you would need to know how to say the plural for the item. Piva is the plural of pivo)

(Czech numbers change form in interesting and mysterious ways which we will explore in Section III. There you will learn why we used jedno instead of jeden, the way the number one appears in the number list on the preceding page)

For now, imagine that you are shopping in one of Prague's many small grocery stores called a potraviny. Ask the store clerk for the following items in the glass display behind the counter:

This is how you would say, "Good day. I would like three cokes please."

Good Day= dobrý den

I would like= Dám si or Já si dám (literally, I will give myself)

three cokes, please.= kola, tři krát, prosím.

Expressions of Quantity

In the Language Brain in Section II, you will see a heading there called Quantifiers. The words listed there are expressions of quantity such as, a lot, many, most, etc.. We often use the word *of* after many of these types of quantifying words, as in, A lot *of* people will be there or many of these, etc..Czech achieves this idea through grammatical changes in the words without the use of the word *of*. For our Bad Czech purposes, we will simply omit the word *of* when translating to Czech. You would just say, "A lot people" For example: A lot people are here =.**Tady je hodně lidí. Hodně is the word for** *a lot* **in Czech.**

Telling Time (part 1)

"The Plane leaves at 1:35 p.m.

We've learned how to ask for the time but we haven't learned how to tell someone the time in Czech. Here, we will learn how to say the time, on the hour, and minutes past, and minutes to the hour. (Saying a quarter past, half-past and a quarter to the hour is explained in section three.)

It is one o'clock.   Je jedna hodina.

It is two o'clock.   Jsou dvě hodiny.

It is three o'clock.   Jsou tři hodiny.

It is four o'clock   Jsou čtyři hodiny.

It is five o'clock   Je pět hodin.

It is six o'clock   Je šest hodin ... and so on up to twelve.

Notice: je is used for one o'clock and from five o'clock up to twelve. Whereas, *jsou* is used for two, three and four o'clock. Also, if you haven't guessed, the word for hour is hodina and its ending changes by dropping the a at the end of the word and adding a y as in dvě hodiny or by dropping the a as in pět hodin. More on these changes later.

Minutes past and minutes to the hour:

Minutes past:

It is ten past seven (It is seven and ten minutes)
Je sedm (hodin) a deset minut.
(You can also say this without *a* (and),
"Je sedm deset")

Minutes to:

It is ten to seven:
Je za deset (minut) sedm (hodin)

(The word *za* has several meanings but here it means to or *towards*)

Language Creation Lab # 10

Telling Time (part 1)

plane=letadlo, leaves = odlétá,   at = v, ve

1)   It's nine o'clock. =

2) It's ten past five. =

3) The plane leaves (departs) at one thirty-five. =
(Answers to Lab # 10 on page 66)

*The preposition *in* can be either v or ve in Czech depending on the pronunciation of the word it precedes. There are no hard and fast rules but I have noticed that ve is often used when the word which follows expels air as with words beginning with the letter *s* as in ve sněhu - in the snow, rather than those letters which aspirate as with words beginning with p, as in, v parku - in the park.

*Europe runs on the twenty-four hour clock system. Consequently, you will often hear the time given in this way. Thus, 2:00 p.m. can be said as two o'clock-dvě hodiny or 14:00, which is fourteen o'clock—čtrnáct hodin. In context, you will be understood whichever method you use.

Calendar Time

Days

Monday	pondělí (n)
Tuesday	úterý (n)
Wednesday	středa (f)
Thursday	čtvrtek (m)
Friday	pátek (m)
Saturday	sobota (f)
Sunday	neděle (f)

*Czech days and months are not usually capitalized.

Months

January	leden
February	únor
March	březen
April	duben
May	květen
June	červen
July	červenec
August	srpen
September	září
October	říjen
November	listopad
December	prosinec

Lab #10 Answers

1. It's nine o'clock. = Je devět hodin.

2. It's ten past five. = Je pět deset

3. The plane leaves (departs) at one thirty-five. = Letadlo odlétá ve třináct třicet pět.

Ordinal Numbers

1st	první		16th	šestnáctý
2nd	druhý		17th	sedmnáctý
3rd	třetí		18th	osmnáctý
4th	čtvrtý		19th	devatenáctý
5th	pátý		20th	dvacátý
6th	šestý		21st	dvacátý první
7th	sedmý		22nd	dvacátý druhý
8th	osmý		23rd	dvacátý třetí
9th	devátý		24th	dvacátý čtvrtý
10th	desátý		25th	dvacátý pátý
11th	jedenáctý		26th	dvacátý šestý
12th	dvanáctý		27th	dvacátý sedmý
13th	třináctý		28th	dvacátý osmý
14th	čtrnáctý		29th	dvacátý devátý
15th	patnáctý		30th	třicátý
			31st	třicátý první

What's the date today? Kolikátého je dnes? Part 1

In English, you could respond to the above question in one of two ways:

You could say : "It's October 22nd" or "It's the 22nd of October."

Here we will learn how to say the first variation and in Section III, the second version, which requires more steps.

By looking at the ordinal numbers chart, we can say the date using the first variation as we do in English.

Thus: It is October twenty-second = Je řijen dvacátý druhý.(the more common word order places the month at the end of the sentence, as in, Je dvacátý druhý řijen.

Now you try:

Language Creation Lab #11
Saying the Date

1. It's January 23rd =
2. It's September 5th =
3. It's May 21st =

(Answers to Lab # 11 and 12 on page 71)

Expressing Likes and Dislikes
"I like chocolate."

Two words are commonly used to express "likes" in Czech. The word rád means to enjoy, like or love. It combines with the verb have to express likes and dislikes. The infinitive of have is mít. From it we can form I have=mám, you have=máš, etc. As mentioned earlier, you can learn the rules for creating the various verb forms in Section III. For your convenience, the *I* and *you* forms are provided for you here in the examples.

I like chocolate = Mám rád čokoládu.*
I don't like chocolate = Nemám rád čokoládu.*

(Male and female differences are observed here, so if you are a female you would add an a to the end of rád say, "Mám ráda čokoládu")

Do you like chocolate? = Máš rád čokoládu?

You can also use rád to say you like doing something, as in:

I like playing tennis.= Hraju rád tenis. or Rád hraju tenis. (You will learn how it is possible to change the word order in Czech depending on which element in the sentence you want to emphasize.)

For this you will need to learn how to create "I play, or I am playing". See section III page 172.

Czech also uses the verb *líbit se* to express likes for more specifics about things or people. You can say, "I like the taste of chocolate," for example using *líbit se* and say, "Líbí se mi chuť čokolády." A reasonable translation in English would be, "The taste of chocolate is likeable to me." Czech uses the third case form *mi* in this sentence which is almost identical in sound and spelling to the English *me*. You will learn about grammatical cases in Section III.

There are no hard rules for knowing when to use rád or líbit se. All languages have nuances that can only be learned through immersion in the culture and language. I actually wish English had another word for *like* which we could substitute for *love,* which I think we overuse in English. Czech has another word for love which is *milovat,* which is reserved mostly for people and you had better mean it when you say it. ;-)

Language Creation Lab #12

Vocabulary: pie = koláč. ice cream = zmrzlina, but = ale, cake = dort, tennis = tenis, sardines = sardinky,

---

1. I like pie and ice cream but I don't like cake. =
2. Do you like playing tennis? =
3. I don't like sardines =

No if's, and's or but's

Connecting Words

Connecting words, otherwise known as conjunctions, are powerful language engine words and fortunately, they are very easy to use.

In any language, connecting words allow you to string together more than one thought or sentence. They require very little explanation and you can use them the same way you do in English.

The most common connecting words are as follows:

and = a
but = ale
also = taky
or = nebo
because = protože
then (as in, after that) = potom
if = jestli

(Czech has another word for *if* when making a conditional statement, such as, "If I were you, I would tell her," which will be explored in Section III) Jestli is used in the present and future, such as, "We can go there, if you want." or "If I see him, I will tell him.")

Lab #11 Answers

1. It's January 23rd   = Je dvacátého třetího ledna.

2. It's September 5th = Je pátého září.

3. It's May 21st   = Je dvacátého prvního května.

Lab #12 Answers

1. I like pie and ice cream but I don't like cake. =
   Mám rád koláče a zmrzlinu, ale nemám rád dorty.
2. Do you like playing tennis? = Hraješ rád tenis?
3. I don't like sardines = Nemám rád sardinky.

Prepositions

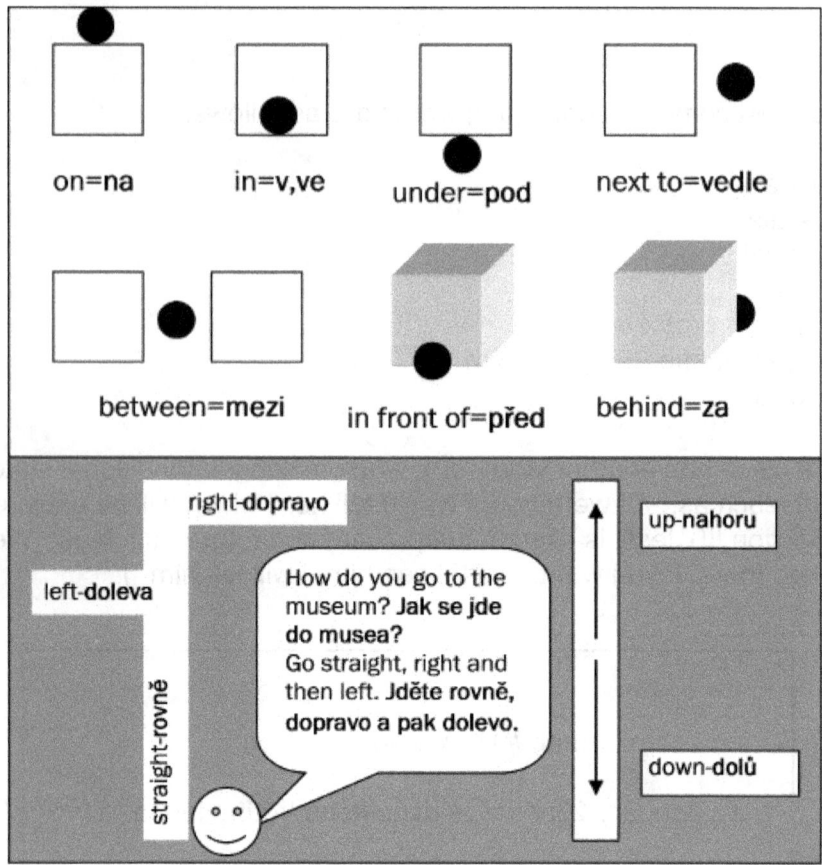

Czech makes a distinction between movement in the direction toward or from a location and the static location. The words change form to indicate the difference. For example: If I say, "I am going up." (movement) vs It is up on the third floor (static). The word *up* changes form to show the difference.

nahoru vs. nahoře

I am going up. (movement) vs. It is up on the third floor (static) Jdu *nahoru* vs. Je to *nahoře* ve třetím poschodí.

Prepositions

As mentioned before, every language uses prepositions idiosyncratically. Therefore, most uses need to be learned individually. For instance, where English uses only the preposition *for* in each of the examples below, Czech uses a different preposition.

This is for you.   To je **pro** tebe.

He asked for help.   Zeptal se **o** pomoc.

I use carrots for cooking.   Pouziji mrkev **na** vaření.

Thanks for the coffee.   Diky **za** kávu.

This is used for tennis.   Toto se používá **k** tenisu.

Prepositions of Location

The book is on the box. The book is between the boxes.

on/off-na-pryč

under / pod

above / nad

over / přes

in front of / před

opposite / naproti

on the left side of – na levé straně od

on the right side – na pravé straně

up/down – nahoru/dolů

into/out of v / vně

inside/outside - vevnitř/ venku

next to = vedle

near/far = blízko-daleko

behind = za

in front of = před

opposite = naproti

on the left side of = na levé straně

on the right side = na pravé straně

Prepositions of Directions

to = do

from the direction of or out of --z, (ze)

from your mother-od tvé matky

from 9 to 5- od 9 do 5

up/down = nahoru/dolů

into/out of = do/z

Prepositions of Relationships

about - o This book is about dogs.

of (unbreakable relationship) This is a map of China. = To je mapa Číny (see Genitive page145)

for - pro
with - s,(se)
without - bez

Se

Other languages use some language features much more often than we do in English.

In Czech, this is particularly true with how the ideas of myself, yourself, ourselves, etc, are expressed and with the frequency of their use.

In English, we could say, "He is getting ready for the big day," or "He is getting himself ready for the big day," with the same meaning. The words himself, yourself, themselves, etc., are called reflexive pronouns.

Czech uses this reflexive pronoun idea very often in many situations where we don't use it, including some basic ones such as:

How are you? Jak se máte?

The reflexive word in this question is *se*. (A semi-literal translation could be, "How are you having yourself?")

And in the answer:
    I am well.   Mám se dobře.
(and this semi-literally means, "I am having myself well.")

We will explore further the use of *se* and its counter parts *si* and *sebe* in Section III.

Czech This Out!

For a country of only 10 million people, The Czech Republic has produced more than its fair share of sport legends and championship teams.

This impressive short list includes Jan Železný, the greatest javelin thrower of all-time.

Ivan Lendl held the number one spot in tennis for five years which places him in an elite group which includes, Connors, McEnroe, Federer and Sampras.

Roman Šebrle was named the world's greatest athlete. He was the Olympic Gold decathalon winner in 2004.

Dominik Hašek is in contention for the greatest NHL goaltender in history.

Martina Navrátilová is considered the greatest singles, doubles and mixed doubles tennis player who's ever lived.

Hockey player Jaromír Jágr is the highest scoring European in NHL history.

Pavel Nedvěd is widely regarded as one of the finest midfielder footballers (soccer players) of the modern era.

The Czech men's national ice hockey team is a member of the so-called "Big Six", the unofficial group of the six strongest men's ice hockey nations. Their accomplishments include an Olympic Gold and several World Championship golds.

It's hard to explain how such a small population pool can produce such extraordinary athletic prowess. Some say it's the beer, I think it's the mushrooms.

Section II

The Czech Language Brain and Conversation Maker

The Czech Language Brain and Conversation Maker contains a summary of much of what you have learned so far.

Once you learn how to pronounce written Czech words, you could just use this section when you are in a cafe or pub to make instant conversation with a new Czech friend. You can mix and match, plug-in and add-on words, expressions and phrases to say almost anything you want. You could print or copy this section and take it with you, to avoid carrying the whole book, see the printing tips below.

And if you can't think of what to say, The Conversation Maker on page 115 has ready to use dialogues that you can use to get acquainted with your new Czech friends.

Printing or copying tips: When printing from the downloadable PDF file, choose "spread" setting and landscape settings on your printer, which will print pages side by side. If you are really savvy, you can print on the front and back as well, then only nine sheets of paper will be required to print this entire section. If copying, reduce the image size on the copy machine to 90% which will fit two side by side pages onto one copied page.

10 Communication Tricks

1. Many word combinations and expressions often make no sense at all when translated directly from one language into another. This is especially true of slang or idioms, or phrasal verbs which are word combinations like get on, take out, give up, etc. More exact words usually exist. For example, you should use *surrender* instead of *give up*, which makes no sense if translated literally.

These word combinations, more often than not, make absolutely no sense translated literally into another language. Similarly, some words like *get* have multiple meanings. For example, *get* can mean to receive or obtain but it can also mean to arrive, as in 'We got there at 7 o'clock'.

2. Czech doesn't use articles like a, an or the. (However, do note that often the words this or that can substitute for the word the. For example, You could say, "Who is *that* man standing by the door?" Instead of "Who is *the* man standing by the door?" with little change in meaning. So, in Czech you can use the word *ten* in these situations. Also, sometimes in English we say, there is *some* man waiting for you in the lobby, instead of *a* man. In similar type sentences you can use the word nějaký in Czech.

3. As you learned earlier, Czech does not use the helping words *do* or *does* but simply uses rising intonation to make the question and precedes the verb with the suffix *ne* to make the negative.

4. If you don't know the tenses, learn how to say yesterday-včera, and tomorrow-zítra, and other time words. Then use only the present tense and say "Yesterday I dance" or "Tonight I dance", for instance. This is much more understandable than using the wrong tense.

5. If you can't compare adjectives, learn the words more and less and say more good or more fast, etc. The word for more in czech is **více** and less is **méně**.

6. Keep your sentences short and create more sentences.

7. Numbers are universal, you can write them down or ask them to be written down.

8. Be direct: You don't have the language skill to be eloquent, to qualify or beat around the bush. For instance, use the verb want and offer specific suggestions: Do you want pizza or Chinese food? (The top twenty verbs included at the end of the language brain will allow you to get most of your needs met.

9. Leverage the language you know and simplify: Simplify, Simplify, Simplify. Leverage your vocabulary. There is usually a simpler word you can use to get your point across. One source suggests that 20,000 words could be reduced to 800 simpler words to rephrase almost any statement, (excluding the need for specialized words of course). Most of these eight-hundred words are included in this section.

10. Reword your sentences: There is usually more than one way to say virtually the same thing, so don't get attached to trying to say something in a particular way. Again, keep it simple.

1. We mostly make positive and negative statements and questions with subject pronouns with the verb *to be* in the past, present and future.

The Czech People Brain

I = Já
Present—I am—(já) jsem
Past—I was—If you are a man you would say byl jsem
If you are a woman you would say byla jsem
Future—I will be—(já) budu

You = Ty
Present—You are—(ty) jsi
Past—You were—when addressing
a man you would say byl jsi
when addressing a woman you would say byla jsi
Future—You will be—(ty) budeš

He = On
Present—He is—(on) je
Past—He was—byl
Future—He will be—bude

She = Ona
Present—she is—(ona) je
Past—she was—byla
Future—she will be—(ona) bude

Bob = Bob
Bob is—Bob je
Bob was—Bob byl
Bob will be—Bob bude

We = My
Present—We are—(my) jsme
Past—We were—byli jsme
Future—We will be—budeme

You/formal/plural = Vy
Present—You are—(vy) jste
Past—You were—byli jste
Future—You will be—(vy) budete

They = Oni
Present—They are—(oni) jsou
Past—They were—byli
Future—They will be-(oni) budou

It = Ono/to
Present—it is—(ono) je
Past—it was—bylo
Future—it will be—(to) bude

We often say Me a lot.

Mini Me Brain

me-mě
you-tebe
him-ho
it-ho
her-jí
us-nás
them-jim
you (plural)-vás

*with me-se mnou
with you-s tebou

We often say My a lot.

Mini My Brain

my-moje
your-tvoje
his-jeho
its-jeho
her-její
our-naše
their-jejich
your (plural)- vaše

Other people in our lives

People Words

people-lidi
person-člověk
man-muž
men-muži,
woman-žena,

women-ženy
girl-holka
girls-holky, boy-kluk
boys-kluci
child-dítě
children-děti
baby-miminko
friend-kamarád, friends-přátelé, boyfriend-přítel, girlfriend-přítelkyně, husband-manžel wife-manželka, son-syn, daughter-dcera,mother-matka
father-otec
brother-bratr
sister-sestra,
Mr./Sir-Pane
Mrs.-Paní,
Miss-Slečno
family- rodina
parents-rodiče
boss-šéf, ředitel, vedoucí
employee-zaměstnanec
customer-zákazník
client-klient
citizen-občan

Professions/Occupations:
engineer – inženýr
businessman - obchodník
lawyer - právník
doctor - doktor
teacher - učitel
student – student

2. And we make positive and negative statements and questions with subject pronouns with other verbs in the past, present and future.

1. To use verbs in a foreign language you need to know their past, present and future forms or how to form them and other aspects if they exist. For example, English also has the continuous and perfect aspects, as in, He is playing tennis now and he has played tennis before. Not all languages have the twelve which exist in English,

additionally, some languages, like Czech, have other variants as well, which are discussed in Section 3. For the purposes of instant Czech, the most common verbs and their main conjugations, the changes they make, for each person and tense are provided for you here, ready to use.

*Remember, The negative is formed by adding the letters *ne* to the front of the verb.
And the question is formed with the rising intonation technique.
For example: *I want* is *chci* so *I don't want* is *nechci*.
Do you want...? is Chceš?
Easy, huh?

Your First Four Essential Verbs
want, have, go, and can

Your first four essential verbs are **want**, **have**, **go** and **can**. With these starting verbs you can navigate the world. Your life begins with you **wanting** something (a noun) or wanting to do something (another verb), **going** and getting it, and since we often want something from others, we have to ask if we **can** have or do something. And then we **have** what we want.

Verb plus Verb combinations

After some verbs like, *want*, we can add a second verb and make a statement like, "I want *to eat* pizza."

After I want, or you want, etc, the second verb is in its infinitive form, in English as well as in Czech. For example, With the help of "to", We say, "I want to go." Czech does not use *to* but simply uses the verb in its infinitive or how you might find it listed in the dictionary before any grammatical changes are made to it. In the lists found here, the verb is first shown in its infinitive form.

So, to say, "I want to go" Find the verb want on the next page, then find the "I want" form which is Chci. then find the verb *go* which is Jít. Combine the two words which creates "Chci jít". The other most

83

common verb plus verb combinations are created with the verbs Need to, and Have to, which can be found on the next pages.

Conjugations

The past, present and future are given for the first person singular (the I form) for some of the most commonly used verbs. In Section 3 you will learn how to create the full conjugations for all verbs.

Imperfective/Perfective Verb Forms

In the Gold Medal section, you will learn that most Czech verbs have two infinitive forms called the imperfective and perfective. The perfective infinitive has a future tense meaning. In brief, the perfective form indicates a one time action or an action which has been completed, whereas the imperfective shows an action which is more open ended, such as the difference between I will call the client tonight versus I will be calling clients all night. Remember that Czech does not have a separate continuous form of the verb, so "I play tennis," and "I am playing tennis" use the same verb form and only the context would indicate whether the action is taking place now or that you play generally.

In the list of verbs that follows on the next few pages this difference is indicated by the letters I and P in case you make it through Section 3 and want to make use of these two verb forms in the future :-) For now, you can just ignore these abbreviations. Some verbs are more commonly used in one form or the other or only in one form, or with a change in meaning if used in the perfective. Also, some verbs are neither perfective nor imperfective but are a type known in English as modal verbs. This is the reason some verbs are not marked or only one form is given.

Want - Chtít

Present
I want	chci	we want	chceme
you want	chceš	you want	chcete
he,she,it	chce	they want	chtějí

Past
I wanted	chtěl jsem	we wanted	chtěli jsme
you wanted	chtěl jsi	you wanted	chtěli jste
he wanted	chtěl	they wanted	chtěli
she wanted	chtěla		
it wanted	chtělo		

Future
I will want	budu chtít	we will want	budeme chtít
you will want	budeš chtít	you will want	budete chtít
he,she,it	bude chtít	they will want	budou chtít

Have - Mít

Present
I have	mám	we have	máme
you have	máš	you have	máte
he-she-it	má	they have	mají

Past
I had	měl jsem	we had	měli jsme
you had	měl jsi	you had	měl jste
He had	měl	they had	měli
she had	měla		
it had	mělo		

Future
I will have	budu mít	we will have	budeme mít
you will have	budeš mít	you will have	budete mít
he-she-it will	bude mít	they will have	budou mít

Go - Jít (P)

Present

I go	jdu	we go	jdeme
you go	jdeš	you go	jdete
he-she-it	jde	they go	jdou

Past

I went	šel jsem	we went	šli jsme
you went	šel jsi	you went	šli jste
he went	šel	they went	šli
she went	šla		
it went	šlo		

Future

I will go	půjdu	we will go	půjdeme
you will go	půjdeš	you will go	půjdete
he-she-it will go	půjde	they will go	půjdou

Go - Chodit: (I)

Czech has several words for coming and going. Here the verb Chodit is used in the way English would use the simple present or actions we do habitually. Such as, *Every day I go to the gym. = Každý den chodím do posilovny, as opposed to, "I´m going to the store." = Jdu do obchodu, which is something you are doing now or in the future. More examples: "I´m going to the cinema today." = "Dnes jdu do kina", "I go to the cinema every day." = "Chodím do kina každý den."

Present

I go	Chodím	we go	Chodíme
You go	Chodíš	you (plural)	Chodíte

he,she,it go	chodí	they go	chodí

Past

I went	chodil jsem	we went	chodili jsme
You went	chodil jsi	you went	chodili jste
he went	chodil	they went	chodili/y (y is used if all female)
she went	chodila		
it went	chodilo		

Future

I will go	Budu chodit	we will go	Budeme chodit
you will go	Budeš chodit	you will go	Budete chodit (půjdete)
he,she, it will go	Bude chodit	they will go	Budou chodit (půjdou)

Can - Moci

Present

I can	můžu	we can	můžeme
you can	můžeš	you can	můžete
he,she,it	může	they can	můžou

Past

I could	mohl jsem	we could	mohli jsme
you could	mohl jsi	you could	mohli jste
he could	mohl	they could	mohli
she could	mohla		
it could	mohlo		

Future

I will be able to	budu moct	we will be able to	budeme moct
you	budeš moct	you will be able to	budete moct
he,she,it will be able to	bude moct	they will be able to	budou moct

*Remember, the question is formed with the rising intonation technique. Can I? Můžu?

More Common Verbs

Say/Tell - Říkat (I)

Present
I say	říkám	we say	říkáme
you say	říkáš	you say	říkáte
he-she-it	říká	they say	říkají

Past
I said	říkal jsem	we said	říkali jsme
you said	říkal jsi	you said	říkali jste
he said	říkal	they said	říkali
she said	říkala		

Future: Budu řikat

Future
I will say	řeknu	we will say	řekneme
you will say	řekneš	you will say	řeknete
he-she-it	řekne	they will say	řeknou

Say/Tell - Říct (P)

Present
I tell	říkám	we tell	říkáme
You tell	říkáš	you (plural) tell	říkáte
he,she,it tells	říká	they tell	říkají

Past
I told	řekl jsem	we told	řekli jsme
You told	řekl jsi	you told	řekli jste
He told řekl	they told	řekli	
she told řekla			
it told řeklo			

Future
I will tell	Řeknu	we will tell	Řekneme
you will tell	Řekneš	you will tell	Řeknete
he,she,it will tell	Řekne	they willtell	Řeknou

Think - Myslet (I)

Present
I think	myslím	we think	myslíme
you think	myslíš	you think	myslíte
he-she-it	myslí	they think	myslí

Past
I thought	myslel jsem	we thought	mysleli jsme
you thought	myslel jsi	you thought	mysleli jste
he thought	myslel	they thought	mysleli
she thought	myslela		
it thought	myslelo		

Future
I will think	budu myslet	we will think	budeme myslet
you will think	budeš myslet	you will think	budete myslet

Do/Make - Dělat (I)

Present
I do	dělám	we do	děláme
you do	děláš	you do	děláte
he,she,it	dělá	they do	dělají

Past
I did	dělal jsem	we did	dělali jsme
you did	dělal jsi	you did	dělali jste
he did	dělal	they did	dělali
she did	dělala		
it did	dělalo		

Future
I will do	budu dělat	we will do	budeme dělat
you will do	budeš dělat	you will do	budete dělat
he,she,it	bude dělat	they will do	budou dělat

Do/Make - Udělat (Perfective)

Present (the imperfective form of do is used in the present), see above

Past
I did	udělal jsem	we did	udělali jsme
You did	udělal jsi	you did	udělali jste
he did	(on) udělal	they did	(oni) udělali
she did	(ona) udělala		
it did	(ono/to) udělalo		

Future
I will do	udělám	we will do	uděláme
you will do	uděláš	you will do	uděláte
he,she,it will do	udělá	they willdo	udělají

Work - Pracovat (I)

Present
I work	pracuji	we work	pracujeme
you work	pracuješ	you work	pracujete
he,she,it	pracuje	they work	pracují

Past
I worked	pracoval jsem	we worked	pracovali jsme
you worked	pracoval jsi	you worked	pracovali jste
he worked	pracoval	they worked	pracovali
she worked	pracovala		
it worked	pracovalo		

Future
I will work	budu pracovat	we will work	budeme pracovat
you will work	budeš pracovat	you willwork	budete pracovat
he,she,it	bude pracovat	they will work	budou pracovat

to Come - Přijít (P)

Present

I come	přicházím	we come		přicházíme
you come	přicházíš	you come	(plural)	přicházíte
he,she,it comes	přichází	they come		přicházejí

Past

I came	přišel jsem	we came	přišli jsme
you came	přišel jsi	you came	přišli jste
he came	přišel	they came	přišli
she came	přišla		
it did	přišlo		

Future

I will come	přijdu	we will come	přijdeme
you will come	přijdeš	you will come	přijdete
he,she,it will come	přijde	they will come	přijdou

to Come - Přicházet (I)

Present

I come	přicházím	we come	přicházíme
you come	přicházíš	you come (plural)	přicházíte
he,she,it comes	přichází	they come	přicházejí

Past

I came	přicházel jsem	we came	přicházeli jsme
you came	přicházel jsi	you came	přicházeli jste
he came	přicházel	they came	přicházeli
she came	přicházela		
it did	přicházelo		

Future

I will come	budu přicházet	we will come	budeme přicházet
you will come	budeš přicházet	you will come	budete přicházet
he,she,it will come	bude přicházet	they will come	budou přicházet

Know - Vědět

Present
I know	vím	we know	víme
you know	víš	you know	víte
he,she,it	ví	they know	vědí

Past
I knew	věděl jsem	we knew	věděli jsme
you knew	věděl jsi	you knew	věděli jste
he knew	věděl	they knew	věděli
she knew	věděla		
it knew	vědělo		

Future
I will know	budu vědět	we will know	budeme vědět
you will know	budeš vědět	you will know	budete vědět
he,she,it will know	bude vědět	they will know	budou vědět

Have to (must) - Muset

Present
I have to	musím	we have to	musíme
you have to	musíš	you have to	musíte
he,she,it	musí	they have to	musí

Past
I had to	musel jsem	we had to	museli jsme
you had to	musel jsi	you had to	museli jste
he had to	musel	they had to	museli
she had to	musela		
it had to	muselo		

Future
I will have to	budu muset	we will have to	budeme muset
you will have to	budeš muset	you will have to	budete muset
he,she,it will have to	bude muset	they will have to	budou muset

Other Top Verb

Only the first person singular is given here in the present and past, as well as the perfective and imperfective form for some verbs, explained in Section III, page 174. The Czech verb is preceded by (P) for the perfective form and (I) for the imperfective form. Most forms here are in the informal. (See Appendix for the "you" form.) Note: The reflexive particle *se* could be added to most of the verbs here to create the idea of oneself, which is used quite often in Czech. See page 75 and page 214 for more on this.

bring -	(P) přinést	přinesu	přinesl jsem
	(I) nosit	nosím	nosil jsem
buy -	(P) koupit	koupím	koupil jsem
	(I) kupovat	kupuju	kupoval jsem
call -	(P) zavolat	zavolám	zavolal jsem
	(I) volat	volám	volal jsem
cause -	(P) způsobit	způsobím	způsobil jsem
	(I) způsobovat	způsobuju	způsoboval jsem
come -	(P) přijít	přijdu	přišel jsem
	(I) přicházet	přicházím	přicházel jsem
cook -	(P) uvařit	uvařím	uvařil jsem
	(I) vařit	vařím	vařil jsem
dance -	(P) zatancovat	zatancuji	zatancoval jsem
	(I) tancovat	tancuju	tancoval
decide -	(P) rozhodnout	rozhodnu	rozhodl jsem
	(I) rozhodovat	rozhoduju	rozhodoval jsem
do or 'make'-	(P) udělat	udělám	udělal jsem
	(I) dělat	dělám	dělal jsem
drink -	(P) napít	napiju	napil jsem
	(I) pít	piju	pil jsem
drive -	(I) řídit	řídím	řídil jsem

eat -	(P) sníst	sním	snědl jsem
	(I) jíst	jím	jedl jsem
exercise -	(P) zacvičit	zacvičím	zacvičil jsem
	(I) cvičit	cvičím	cvičil jsem
figure out -	(P) vyřešit	vyřeším	vyřešil jsem
	(I) řešit	řeším	řešil jsem
find out -	(P) zjistit	zjistím	zjistil jsem
	(I) zjišťovat	zjišťuji	zjišťoval jsem
forget -	(P) zapomenout	zapomenu	zapomněl jsem
	(I) zapomínat	zapomínám	zapomínal jsem
get/obtain -	(P) dostat	dostanu	dostal jsem
	(I) dostávat	dostávám	dostával jsem
get/become -	(P) stát se	stanu se	stal jsem se
	(I) stávat se	stávám se	stával jsem se
get/arrive -	(P) přijet	přijedu	přijel jsem
	(I) přijíždět	přijíždím	přijížděl jsem
give -	(P) dát	dám	dal jsem
	(I) dávat	dávám	dával jsem
have -	mít	mám	měl jsem
have to -	muset	musím	musel jsem
know -	vědět	vím	věděl jsem
laugh -	(P) zasmát se	zasměju se	zasmál jsem se
	(I) smát se	směju se	smál jsem se
learn -	(P) naučit	naučím	naučil jsem
	(I) učit	učím	učil jsem

leave -	nechat	nechám	nechával jsem
leave (depart) -	(P) odejít	odejdu	odešel jsem
	(I) odcházet	odcházím	odcházel jsem
listen -	(P) poslechnout	poslechnu	poslechl jsem
	(I) poslouchat	poslouchám	poslouchal jsem
look for -	hledat	hledám	hledal jsem
*look -	(P) podívat se	podívám se	podíval jsem se
	(I) dívat se	dívám se	díval jsem se
make/do -	(P) udělat	udělám	udělal jsem
	(I) dělat	dělám	dělal jsem
need -	potřebovat	potřebuju	potřeboval jsem
paint -	(P) namalovat	namaluju	namaloval jsem
	(I) malovat	maluju	maloval jsem
pay -	(P) zaplatit	zaplatím	zaplatil jsem
	(I) platit	platím	platil jsem
play -	(P) zahrát	zahraju	zahrál jsem
	(I) hrát	hraju	hrál jsem
put -	(P) položit	položím	položil jsem
	(I) pokládat	pokládám	pokládal jsem
read	(P) přečíst	přečtu	přečetl jsem
	(I) číst	čtu	četl jsem

* see page 230 for the verb *look* when it is used like the verb *seem or appear* in English, as in, "You look tired."

rest -	(P) odpočinout	odpočinu	odpočinul jsem
	(I) odpočívat	odpočívám	odpočíval jsem
remember -	(P) zapamatovat si	zapamatuju si	zapamatoval jsem si
	(I) pamatovat si	pomatuju si	pamatoval jsem si
say/tell -	(P) říci	řeknu	řekl jsem
	(I) říkat	říkám	říkal jsem
see -	(P) uvidět	uvidím	uviděl jsem
	(I) vidět	vidím	viděl jsem
sell -	(P) prodat	prodám	prodal jsem
	(I) prodávat	prodávám	prodával jsem
send -	(P) poslat	pošlu	poslal jsem
	(I) posílat	posílám	posílal jsem
shop -	(P) nakoupit	nakoupím	nakoupil jsem
	(I) nakupovat	nakupuju	nakupoval jsem
sit -	(P) sednout	sednu	sedl jsem
	(I) sedět	sedím	seděl jsem
sleep -	spát	spím	spal jsem
smile -	(P) usmívat se	usmívám se/směju se	usmál jsem se
	(I) usmát se	usměju se	usmál jsem se
stand -	(P) postavit	postavím	postavil
	(P) stát	stojím	stál
study -	(P) nastudovat	nastuduju	nastudoval jsem
	(I) studovat	studuju	studoval jsem
talk/speak -	(P) promluvit	promluvím	promluvil jsem
	(I) mluvit	mluvím	mluvil jsem

teach -	(P) naučit (I) učit	naučím učím	naučil jsem učil jsem
think -	(I) myslet	myslím	myslel jsem
try -	(P) zkusit (I) zkoušet	zkusím zkouším	zkusil jsem zkoušel jsem
understand -	(P) porozumět (I) rozumět	porozumím (future) rozumím (present)	porozuměl jsem rozuměl jsem
use -	(P) použít (I) používat	použiju (future) používám (present)	použil jsem používal jsem
wait -	(P) počkat (I) čekat	počkám (future) čekám (present)	počkal jsem čekal jsem
walk -	(P) projít se (I) procházet se	projdu se procházím se	prošel jsem se procházel jsem se
want -	chtít	chci	chtěl jsem
wash -	(P) umýt (I) mýt	umyju myju	umyl jsem myl jsem
watch -	(P) podívat se (I) dívat se	podívám se dívám se	podíval jsem se díval jsem se
work -	(I) pracovat	pracuju	pracoval
write -	(P) napsat (I) psát	napíšu píšu	napsal jsem si psal jsem

3. We often say Where and When we are doing, did or are going to do something.

Where phrases

Where Indefinite

everywhere-všude
somewhere-někde
nowhere-nikde
here tady
there-tam
over there-tamhle
outside-venku
inside-uvnitř

At home

at home-doma
in the-v
kitchen-v kuchyni
living room-v obýváku
bedroom-v ložnici
bathroom-v koupelně
garage-v garáži

Out and About

at the corner of-na rohu čeho
in the bus-v autobuse
in the car-v autě
on the street-na ulice
in the plane-v letadle
in the taxi-v taxiku
in the train-ve vlaku
in the tram-v tramvaji

in Prague- v Praze
in America- v Americe

Where at the/in the

at the bank-v bance
on/at beach - na pláži
in the bookstore-v knihkupectví
at bus station - na autobusové zastávce
at Charles square- na Karlově náměstí
at church-v kostele
at cinema-v kině
pharmacy - v lékárně
fitness center-ve fitness centru
florist-v květinářství
gas station-u benzinové pumpy
grocery store-v potravinách
hospital-v nemocnici
library- v knihovně
metro-v metru
metro platform-na nástupišti
nature-v přírodě
ocean-v oceánu
office-v kanceláři
park-v parku
parking lot-na parkovišti
police station-na policii
post office-na poště
restaurant-v restauraci
school-ve škole
sea-u moře
sky- na obloze
store-v obchodě
supermarket-v supermarketu
at the theater-v divadle
at the train station-na nádraží
at the tram stop-na zastávce
in the water- ve vodě
at work-v práci

When phrases

Today/Present

today-dnes
now-teď
this time-tentokrát
sometime-někdy
someday-někdy
tonight-večer
this morning- dnes ráno
in the morning-ráno
this afternoon- dnes odpoledne
this evening-dnes večer

When
Yesterday/Past

yesterday-včera
before-předtím, před, dříve
early-časně, brzy
earlier-dříve
2 minutes ago-před dvěma minutami
2 days ago-před dvěma dny
2 weeks ago-před dvěma týdny
2 years ago-před dvěma roky
many years ago-před mnoha roky
last time-naposledy
last night-včera večer
last week-minulý týden
the week before last-předminulý týden
last year-minulý rok
in the past-v minulosti
a long time ago-před mnoha lety
at that time(then)-tehdy
at 3 o'clock-ve tři hodiny
on Friday-v pátek
another time-jindy
in September-v září
that night-tu noc

When
Tomorrow/Future

tomorrow-zítra
the day after tomorrow-pozítří
later-později
after-potom
afterwards-později
next time-příště
next week-příští týden
next year-příští rok
the week after next-přes příští týden
in 5 min.-za pět minut
in 1 year-za rok (za jeden rok)
in the future-v budoucnosti
this weekend-tenhle víkend

How often?

always-vždy, stále
sometimes-občas
never-nikdy
usually-obvykle
everyday-každý den
everytime-pokaždé
once/twice/three times a day/
week/year-jednou/dvakrát/třikrát
za den/týden/rok

How Long?

all day-celý den
for five minutes-pět minut
during-během
soon-brzo
until-dokdy, až do
already-už
since 3 o'clock-od 3 hodin

I am at, I was at, I will be at, I am going to
Quite often where we say I went someplace, Czechs say I was at someplace. So, instead of saying you went to the cinema last night, say you were at the cinema last night.

4. Making questions with Who, what, when, where, why, how, why, whose and which.

Notice how Czech has a single question word to ask, Where you are going, where you are from, how many and what kind of.

Who=Kdo Who is that? Kdo je to?	**What=Co** What is that? Co je to?	**When=Kdy** When does it start? Kdy to začíná?
Where=Kde Where is the castle? Kde jsou Hradčany?	**Why=Proč** Why not? Proč ne?	**How=Jak** How old is it? Jak je to staré?
To Where=Kam Where are you going? Kam jdeš?		**From Where=Odkud** Where are you from? Odkud jste?
Which=*Který Which one is better? Který je lepší?		**How much/many=Kolik** How much is it? Kolik to stojí?
Whose = Čí Whose pen is this? Čí je to pero?		**What kind of=*Jaký** What kind of films do you like? Jaké filmy se ti líbí?

In Section III, we will see other variations of *what* and *who*.

Requests and Offers

Requests

I would like a cola, please. Dal bych si kolu, prosím.
Easy variation: one coke, please - Jednu kolu, prosím.

I would like to order. - Chtěl bych si objednat, prosím.
We would like to order. - Chtěli bychom si objednat, prosím.
(I would like to make an appointment) Rád bych si domluvil schůzku.

Could you close the window, please? Můžeš zavřít okno?
Mohl(a) bys zavřít okno? (polite)

Could you give me a fork, please? Mohl byste mi dát vidličku, prosím?

Offers

Would you like some water? Dáš si vodu?

Permission

Can I shut the window? Můžu zavřít okno?
(The verb following the verb can is in the infinitive form.)

Invitations

Would you like to go to the cinema? Chceš jít do kina?
Chtěl(a) bys jít do kina? (polite)

5. We often say "There is or There are..." Je — Jsou

We often say, *There is* or *There are*. Czech doesn't have unique words for there is and there are but instead simply uses the verbs *is* and *are* alone to convey the same meaning.

There is a metro in Prague. = V Praze je metro.
There are pubs here. = Tady jsou hospody.

At times, you may want to make more clear the existence or presence of something. For these instances, you can say *existuje*, which translates as, there exists.

6. We often say "This, That, These or Those." "ten/to, tamto, tyto, tamty"

EX: This pencil, These pencils. That pencil, Those pencils. Although the difference between this and that is not as pronounced in Czech, it does have many more "pointing" words, i.e., ten, ta, to, tento, tom, tuto, tenhle, těch, to name a few. We will be understood however, if we use *to* for this, to or tamto for that, *tyto* for these and *tamty* for those.

7. We often say "of"

EX: A map of China. A glass of milk. etc. Czech does not have an equivalent word for of but instead changes the form of the words to show this meaning. We will simply omit the word *of* when speaking. So, a map of China becomes mapa Číny in Instant Czech. (later you will learn that číny is the correct form of china to use here)

8. We say, "the man who or that, or the thing which or that."   Který

EX: The man *who/that* lives next door is rich. The movie *which* we saw last night was good. Czech has many variations of these words but we will be understood if we just use the word který. Don't worry about it. ;-)

9. He said that... (že)...

We often use the word *that* to connect one thought to another. As in, "He said that he was tired." or "It is so heavy that it can't be moved." The Czech word which is used for this purpose is že. In English, the word *that* can often be omitted but in Czech you should always use it.

10. We say why we do things. because — protože

Several ways exist in English to express why we do something. And of course, there is usually more than one way to express any thought.

In response to the question, "Why are you going to the store?"

We might answer,

1 I am going to the store to buy bread.
2. I am going to the store for bread.
3. I am going to the store so I can buy bread.
4. I am going to the store so that I can buy bread.
5. I am going to the store because I want to buy bread.
6. I want bread. That is why I am going to the store, or that is the reason I am going to the store.

As mentioned before, there is usually more than one way to express a thought in a language, but as a beginner it is best to learn one simple variation that you can use in most situations. For our fast Czech purposes, we will use the word *because* which in Czech is protože. See number 5 above. In the Gold Medal Czech section you will learn other ways to express the reason for doing something.

11. We say how we do things.

Ex: He went by car. How did he go?-by car. He ate with a spoon. How did he eat?-with a spoon.

How we do things can refer to the manner in which something is done, as with the adverbs, carefully or quickly, for example, or the means or method by which something is done, as in, with a spoon or by car. Here we will focus on the second meaning. The Gold Medal Section explores the use of adverbs and how to form them.

We say the word *with* a lot and so do the Czechs. So much so, that Czech changes the words to show when something is done by or with someone or thing, as in the examples above, and in: She is with Bob.

The main word for *with* in Czech is the letter *s*. It also appears as *se* before words beginning with z, to aid listening where the sound would otherwise be lost. (note: the word se has other uses as you learned earlier and will learn more about in Sectiion III)

The Czech word for auto is auto, but when the word *with* (*s*) precedes it, the *o* is dropped and *em* is added to the end of the word which becomes *s autem*, to mean by or with an auto. This happens to words ending in *o*. For words in the singular ending in *a*, the *a* is dropped and an *ou* is added. So, 'with ice cream'-zmrzlina becomes 'se zmrzlinou.' For masculine words ending in consonants, just add em--student becomes studentem. For feminine nouns ending in the letter *t*, as in *bone,* or *kost* in Czech, add the letter long *í,* which becomes *s kostí.* If you forget to do this, don't worry about it. You will still be understood if you remember to say with-s/se before the thing you are talking about.

But do remember to say *with me - se mnou* and *with you - s tebou* and you will be speaking gold medal Czech.

Common Commands

Watch out!	pozor
Be careful	buď opatrný
Be quiet	buď zticha/potichu
Call me	zavolej mi
Come here	pojď sem
Don't worry	neboj se
Give me please...	dejte mi prosim
Go away	jdi pryč
Help!	pomoc!
Hurry up	pospěš si
Kiss me	polib mě/dej mi pusu
Leave me alone	dej mi pokoj
Listen/to this	poslouchej/poslechni si to
Look out	dávej pozor/dávejte pozor
Look/ at this	Podívej/ Podívej se na to
Make	udělej
Meet me	sejdeme se
Say	řekni mi
Send it	pošli to
Show me	ukaž mi
Sit Down	sedni si
Stay	zustaň
Stop that	přestaň
Tell me	řekni mi
Taste this	ochutnej to
Write it down, please	napiš to, prosím
Wait	počkej

*In Section III, you will learn the rules for creating the imperative in Czech.

SPEAK CZECH BADLY! BUT SPEAK IT TODAY!

We often say, I could/would/should...have

Should (advice and expectations)

I should = Měl bych
You should = Měl bys
he should = Měl by
she should = Měla by
it should = Mělo by

We should = Měli bychom
You should = Měli byste

They should = Měli by

I shouldn't (to form the negative simply add the letters 'ne' before the first word, thus: I shouldn't = neměl bych
To make a question, simply use the same word order with a rising intonation: Should I ...?- Měl bych..?

Should + plus the infinitive form of the verb is used to express these ideas, as in English. (See Appendix for male/female differences in the plural)

Should have

Should have-(past advice and expectations)

I should have = Měl jsem
You should have = Měl(a) jsi
he should have= Měl
she should have = Měla
it should have= Mělo

We should have = Měli jsme
You should have= Měli jste

They should have = Měli

negative = I shouldn't have= neměl jsem
yes/no question = Should I have...? same order- měl jsem..?

Could-(Possibilities & polite requests)

I could = mohl bych
you could = mohl bys
he could = mohl by
she could = mohla by
it could = mohlo by

we could = mohli bychom
you could = mohli byste

they could = mohli by

Negative: I couldn't = nemohl bych
Question: Could I ? = Mohl bych..?

Could have - (Past possibility and past ability)

I could have= mohl jsem
you could have= mohl(a) jsi
he could have= mohl
she could have= mohla
it could have= mohlo

we could have= mohli jsme
you could have= mohli jste

they could have= mohli

Negative: I couldn't have = nemohl jsem

Would/would have

(Czech uses would for would have plus context to show the difference)

I would = Já bych
you would = Ty bys
he would = On by
she would = Ona by
it would = ono by or to by

we would = My bychom
you would = Vy byste

they would = Oni by

"If I were rich, I would buy a castle."

If I   Kdybych   If we   kdybychom
If you   kdybys   If you   kdybyste
If he/she/it kdyby   If they kdyby

Kdybych + L verb form, bych + L verb form

Would have

In everyday speech, Czech uses the same form for *would* as for *would have* and lets context distinguish between the present and past. In both instances, the verb which follows is in the past tense.

Language Spark Plugs
The functional words

These functional words are a collection of essential words we need frequently and are used in most sentences. They are words which qualify, quantify and join our ideas together.

Conjunctions

and- **a**
but-**ale**
or-**nebo**
also-**taky**
unfortunately-**bohužel**
fortunately-**naštěstí**
instead of-**místo**
still-**ještě**
then-**potom**
then-**pak**
because-**protože**
otherwise-**jinak**
if-**jestli**
that-**že**

Qualifiers

maybe-možná
very-velmi, moc
only-jenom, pouze
almost-skoro
just-už
already-už
unless- pokud ne
except- kromě
in-v, ve
to-do
at-na
for-pro
with-s, se
without-bez
the same as-stejný jako
different-rozdílný
the difference between- rozdíl mezi
mostly-většinou

Indefinite things

something-něco
nothing-nic
everything-všechno
whatever-cokoli
what else-co ještě

Prepositions	Indefinite quantity
n-/at-v,ve from-od to- do on-na for-pro with-s, se without-bez next-příští here-zde there-tam up-nahoru down-dolů over-přes around-kolem	all-vše,všechno none-žádný more-více less-menší enough-dost,stačí a lot-hodně many/much-mnoho most-většina some-trochu,několik a little-trochu every-každý whole-celý another-další another one-ještě jedno the other-ten druhý first-první last-minulý, poslední enough-dost exact-přesný

Indefinite people	Indefinite place
somebody-někdo everybody-každý (člověk) nobody-nikdo whoever-kdokoli who else-kdo ještě	somewhere-někde nowhere-nikde everywhere-všude wherever-kdekoli where else-kde ještě

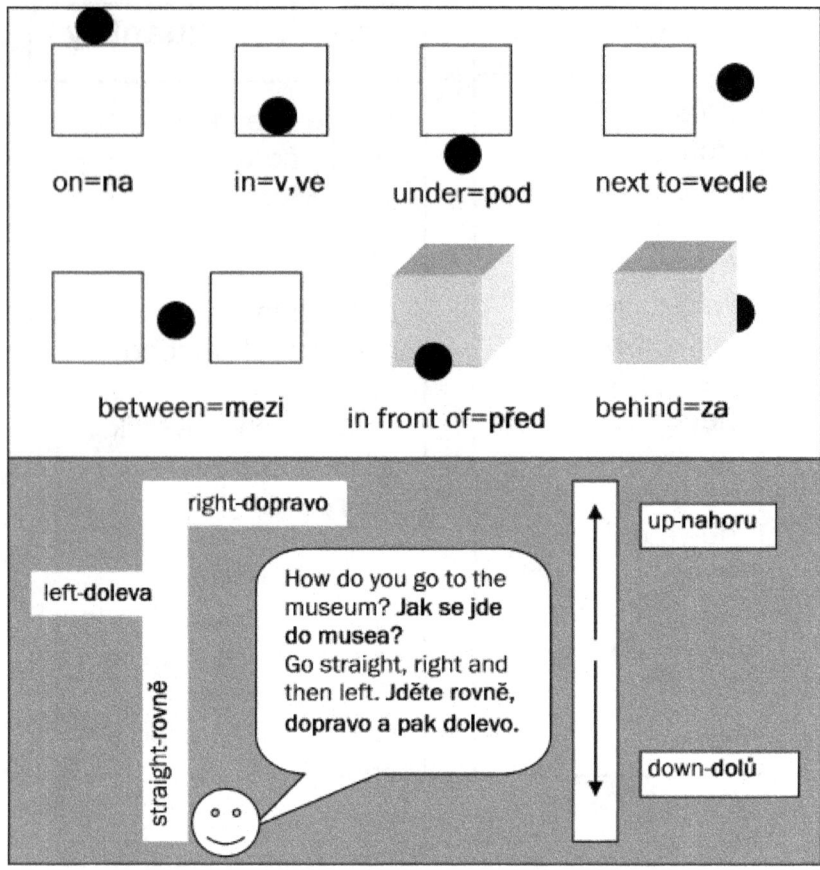

over the bridge-přes most
through the park-skrz park, přes park
under/ pod
above, nad
over- přes
in front of - před
opposite – naproti
on the left side of – na levé straně
on the right side – na pravé straně

up/down – nahoru/dolů

into/out of v / vně

The Nouns we use most
Although there are a large number of total words in a language, we use a surprisingly small number in daily conversation.

The word lists here are not really intended to be used as a dictionary, especially since they are not in alphabetical order. You should read through them to know which words are quickly available to you when making instant conversation in a Czech pub or cafe.

1. People Pronouns: See people brain, mini-me, and my brain. page 80-81.

People

relationship-vztah: people-lidé person-člověk man-muž men-muži, woman-žena, women-ženy girl-holka girls-holky, boy-kluk boys-kluci child-dítě children-děti baby-miminko, friend-kamarád/ka friends-přatelé, boyfriend-přítel, girlfriend-přítelkyně, husband-manžel wife-manželka, son-syn, daughter-dcera, mother-matka, father-otec, brother-bratr, sister-sestra, Mr./Sir-Pán, Mrs.-Paní, Miss-Slečna, family-rodina, boss-šéf, employee - zaměstnanec, customer-zákazník, passenger-cestující, spectator-divák.

Body

body-tělo, head-hlava, face- tvář, eye-oko, eyes-oči, mouth-pusa, lip-ret, nose-nos, ear-ucho, ears-uši, tongue-jazyk, hand-ruka, hands-ruce, foot-chodidlo, feet-chodidla, finger-prst, fingers-prsty, leg-noha, legs-nohy, arm-paže, butt-zadek-prdélka, blood-krev, back-záda, penis-penis, breast-prso, breasts-prsa, vagina-vagina, brain-mozek, heart-srdce, skin-kůže, health - zdraví, disease - nemoc, illness – nemoconemocnění , cough – kašel , sore-throat – bolest v krku, fever (39°C) – horečka, temperature (37,2°C) - teplota, stomachache – bolest břicha, headache – bolest hlavy, toothache - bolest zubů

Clothes

clothes/oblečení: coat-bunda, jacket-kabát, shoes-boty, pants-kalhoty, dress-šaty, socks-ponožky, t-shirt-tričko, suit-backpack-batoh, bag-taška, wallet-peněženka, purse-kabelka, watch-hodinky, razor – břitva/ žiletka(=gillette), toothbrush – zubní kartáček , make-up – make up

Home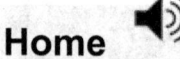

home/ domů-domov, house-dům, flat-byt, room-pokoj, wall-zeď, ceiling-strop floor-podlaha, carpet-koberec, bedroom-ložnice, kitchen-kuchyň, bathroom-koupelna, sink- umyvadlo-dřez, sofa-pohovka, toilet-toaleta, shower-sprcha, door-dveře, window-okno, table-stůl, chair-židle, bed-postel, refrigerator-lednička, washing machine-pračka, curtains-záclony, picture-obraz, garage - garáž, garden - zahrada, balcony - balkón, key - klíč,

Food

food-jídlo, meat-maso, fruit-ovoce, vegetables-zelenina, milk- mléko-
eggs- vajíčka, bread-chleba, cheese - sýr, yogurt - jogurt, soup - polévka, fork - vidlička, spoon - lžíce, knife - nůž, glass - sklenice, cup – hrnek, napkin - ubrousek, bowl – miska/mísa, salt-sůl, pepper- pepř, fresh - čerstvý, ice - led, bottle - láhev, coffee - káva, tea - čaj, beer – pivo , wine - víno,

Work/School

work/school práce/škola, office-kancelář , classroom-třída, desk-psací stůl, paper-papír, pencil-tužka, pen-pero, scissors-nůžky, stapler-sešívačka, computer-počítač, monitor - obrazovka-, keyboard - klávesnice, adhesive tape-lepicí páska, fax-fax, telephone-telefon, building-budova, university-univerzita, note - poznámka, book - kniha, magazine-časopis, envelope- obálka, letter- dopis, stamp- známka.

Transport/Travel

transport/travel: transport-doprava, travel-cestování, car-auto, bus-autobus, tram-tramvaj, metro-metro, train-vlak, plane/jet-letadlo, airport-letiště, main train station-hlavní vlakové nádraží, bus stop-tramvajová zastávka, bicycle-kolo, motorcycle-motorka, scooter – skútr, ship/boat-, taxi-taxi

Money

money-peníze: cash-hotovost, coins-mince, change-drobné, bills-bankovky, price-cena, value-hodnota, worth-hodnota, credit card-kreditní karta, bank-banka

Animals-Insects

animals-insects: animal-zvíře, animals-zvířata, insects-hmyz, dog-pes, cat-kočka, bird-pták, fish-ryba, spider-pavouk, fly-moucha, mosquito-komar,

Nature

nature-příroda, universe-vesmír, outer-space-vesmír, Sun-slunce, moon-měsíc, earth-země, star-hvězda, planet-planeta, cloud-oblak, sky-obloha, air-vzduch, mountain-hora, ocean-oceán, sea-moře, beach-pláž, river-řeka, lake-jezero, stream-potok, tree-strom, flower-květina, plant-rostlina, wind-vítr, fire-oheň, rain-déšť, snow-sníh, weather-počasi, environment-prostředí, animal-zvíře, dog-pes, cat-kočka, bird-pták, insect-hmyz, ground-země, dirt/soil-hlína, mud-bláto, smoke-kouř, temperature-teplota, grass-tráva, garden-zahrada, rock-skála, stone-kámen, sand-písek, fish-ryba, reptile-plaz, lizard-ještěr, snake-had

Culture

culture-kultura, book-kniha, music-hudba, cassette-kazeta, cd-cédečko/ kompaktní disk, cd player-CD přehrávač, computer-počítač, magazine-časopis, newspaper-noviny, dictionary-slovník, library-knihovna, theater-divadlo, opera-opera, art-umění,TV-televize, cinema-kino, film-film, radio-radio, tape player-kazeťák, dance-tanec, ballet-balet, orchestra-orchestr, symphony-symfonie, musician-hudebník, literature-literatura, classic-klasická, architecture-architektura, law-zákon, court-dvůr, lawyer-právík, history-historie, science-věda, philosophy-filosofie, religion-náboženství, mathematics-matematika, politics-politika, communications-komunikace, police-policie, military-armada, mobile phone-mobílní telefon, psychology-psychologie.

Abstract Words

abstract words- abstrakní slova: thing - věc, things - věci, subject – předmět, field - pole, area - oblast, question - otázka, answer - odpověď, idea - myšlenka, discover - objevit, consider (v)– uvážit/posoudit, determine (v) – stanovit/určit, dream - sen, word - slovo, conversation - rozhovor, language - jazyk, pronunciation - výslovnost, cause – příčina/důvod, life - život, death - smrt, information - informace, waste - odpad, useful - užitečný, time - čas, news –novinky, love - láska, beauty - krása, knowledge - znalost, education - vzdělání

Top Adjectives
We often describe people, places and things.

able	schopný
afraid	obávát se, mít strach
angry	rozzlobený
bad	špatný
beautiful	krásný
best	nejlepší,
better	lepší,
big	velký
black	černý
blue	modrý
broken	zlomený
busy	zaneprázdněný
calm	klidný
cheap	levný
clean	čistý
cold	studený
complex	složity
crazy	bláznivý
dark	tmavý
delicious	výborný
depressed	depresivní
difficult	složitý
dirty	špinavý
dry	suchý
easy	jednoduchý
excellent	výborný
expensive	drahý
fantastic	fantastický
fast	rychlý
fat	tlustý
fresh	čerstvý
friendly	přátelský
funny	legrační,
good	dobrý
great	veliký, skvělý
green	zelený
happy	štastný, veselý
hard	tvrdý
heavy	těžký
hot	horký
hungry	hladový
important	důležitý
light	lehký
light	světlý
long	dlouhý
loud	hlasitý
lucky	štastný
neat	v pořádku
necessary	nezbytný
nervous	nervózní
narrow	úzký/omezený
new	nový
nice	pěkný
old	starý
quiet	tichý
ready	připravený
red	červený
relaxed	uvolněný
repaired	opravený
rotten	shnilý
rough	hrubý
sad	smutný
salty	slaný
short	krátký
simple	snadný, jednoduchý
slow	pomalý
small	malý
smooth	hladký
soft	měkký
sour	kyselý
spicy	pálivý, ostrý
spoiled	rozmazlený
sweet	sladký
tall	vysoký
terrible	hrozný
thick	tlustý
thin	tenký
thirsty	žíznivý
tired	unavený
ugly	ošklivý
warm	teplý
wet	mokrý
white	bílý
wide	široký

The Conversation Maker

The conversation maker consists of a collection of social functions and conversation topics to help you make instant conversation. With the exception of greetings and introductions, which typically consist of a few standard expressions, the other topic areas allow you to plug in an array of items into the sentence patterns in the speech bubbles.

Hello's and Goodbye's

Hello, my name's Bob.
What's your name?
Ahoj, jsem Bob.
Jak se jmenuješ?

I'm Monica.
Nice to meet you.
Já jsem Monica.
Těší mě.

Where are you from?
Odkud jste?
I'm from San Francisco.
Jsem ze San Franciska.

Good bye.
Nashledanou
It was nice meeting you!
Těšilo mě

How are you - **Jak se máš?**
I am fine. - **Mám se dobře.**
not bad - **jde to**
And you? - **A ty?**

More Basic Phrases

Hello (to friends) - Ahoj, or čau, or Nazdar,

to strangers and friends - Good day- Dobrý den

Goodbye to friends - čau,

(you will sometimes hear, *Sbohem* which means, with God.)

to strangers and friends-Nashledanou

Good Day- Dobrý Den

Good Evening-Dobrý Večer

Good Night-Dobrou Noc

Yes-ano

No- ne

Thank you- děkuju

Thanks-díky, dík

You're welcome- není zač

literally (It goes) - jde to not bad, so so

What's your name? jak se jmenujete?

My name is... jmenuji se...

Where are you from? odkud jste?

I'm from... Já jsem z...

Pleased to meet you- těší mě

2. People to see

Are you married?
Jsi ženatý/vdaná?

No, I'm single.
Ne, jsem svobodný.

Do you have children?
Máte děti?

Yes, I do. No, I don't.
Ano, mám. Ne, nemám.

Do you have any brothers or sisters/siblings?
Máte nějaké bratry nebo sestry.

Yes, I have one brother and one sister.
Ano, mám jednoho bratra a jednu sestru.

What do you do?
Co děláte?

I'm a student, teacher, businessman, salesperson, etc.
Jsem student, učitel, podnikatel, obchodník atd.

People Words
people-lidé
person-člověk
man-muž
men-muži,
woman-žena,
women-ženy
girl-holka
girls-holky, boy-kluk
boys-kluci
child-dítě
children-děti

baby-miminko
friend-kamarád
friends-přatelé,
boyfriend-přítel,
girlfriend-přítelkyně,
husband-manžel
wife-manželka,
son-syn
daughter-dcera
mother-matka
father-otec

brother-bratr
sister-sestra,
Mr./Sir-Pán
Mrs.-Paní,
Miss-Slečna
family- rodina
parents- rodiče
boss - šéf,
employee - zaměstnanec

Places to go-Things to do

Have you ever been to Paris?
Byl jste někdy v Paříži?

Can you recommend a good nature spot?
Můžete doporučit nějaké dobré přírodní místo?

What do you want to do? **Co chcete dělat?**

Why don't we go to..(the literal translation would have a different meaning in Czech. Better is to use *Let's go to...*)
Pojď'me na... (use *na* for an event like dinner and Pojď'me do... as in *to* the park.

I would rather...
Raději bych...

First we went to... and then...finally
Nejprve jsme jeli do... a potom....nakonec

How did you like it?
Jak se vám to líbilo?

More Places to Go!
café - **kavárna,**
bookstore - **knihkupectví,**
music store - **hudební obchod**
clothes shopping - **nákup oblečení,**
food shopping - **nákup jídla,**
drug store - **drogerie**
pharmacy - **lékárna,**
restaurant - **restaurace,**
walk the streets - **procházet se po ulicích,**
walk in the park - **procházet se v parku,**
go hike in nature -
jít na túru do přírody,
picnic - **piknik,**
music concert - **hudba koncert,**

More Activities

performance - **vystoupení**
poetry readings - **čtení poezie**
theater - **divadlo**
disco dancing - **disco tanec**
night clubs - **noční kluby**
dance lessons - **lekce tance**
performance - **taneční vystoupení**
Latin dance - **latinsko americký tanec**
ball room dancing - **klasický tanec**
sporting event - **sportovní akce,**
movies/cinema/film - **filmy, kino, film**
wedding - **svatba**
party - **party**
internet - **internet**
beer garden - **letní zahrádka**
pubs - **hospody**
sports - **sporty**
games - **hry**
fitness center - **fitness centrum**
swimming - **plavání**
sunbathing - **opalování**
ping pong - **stolní tenis**
chess - **šachy**
tennis - **tenis**
squash - **squash**
exhibits - **výstavy**
museums - **muzea**
galleries - **galerie**
TV video rental - **video půjčovna**

Eating Out

Waiter,Waitress-Menu, please!
(Číšníku, servírko) Prosím jídelní lístek!

Have you chosen?
Máte vybráno?

I will have...cola, beer, red/white wine. 2 dcl, 3 dcl
Dám si... kolu, pivo, červené/bílé víno. 2 deci, 3 deci

This is not what we ordered?
Toto jsme si neobjednali.
There is a mistake. **Tady je chyba.**

Could you bring me...another beer, a fork, a napkin?
Mohl byste mi přinést další pivo, vidličku, ubrousek?

Check, please
Prosím účet
Keep the change.
Drobné si nechte

See you. **Na shledanou**

Could you show me that...? **Mohl byste mi ukázat tamten...?**
How much for that..? Kolik stojí tamten...?
How much for this umbrella? **Kolik stojí tento deštník?**
I would like two of these. **Chtěl bych tyto dva.**
This doesn't fit me, could I exchange it? **To mi nesedí, mohl bych to vyměnit?**
Ok, I'll take it. **Dobře, vezmu si to.**

3. Likes and Dislikes

Do you like pizza?
Chutná Vám pizza?

Me too.
Mně také
I like pizza.
Mám ráda pizzu.

What kind of ___ do you like?
Jaká pizza vám chutná?

Do you know the book, band, film?
Znáš tu knihu, skupinu, film?

What is your favorite___? Jaký je váš oblíbený.....
Who is your favorite___? **Kdo je váš oblíbený**.......

I like...**Mám rád**...
My favorite..is **Můj oblíbený.... je**
I prefer... **dávám přednost...**

Music-rock - hudba rock,
classical - klasika
jazz - jazz
music group - hudební skupina,
rock star - rocková hvězda
Films - filmy
actor - herec
foreign film - zahraniční film
independent - nezávislý
action - akční
horror - horor
thriller - thriller?

Books - knihy
Food - jídlo
Chinese - čínské
Italian - italské
Drink - pití
Beer - pivo
red wine - červené víno,
white wine - bílé víno
Sports - sporty
Games - hry
Dance - tanec

The Universal Pick-up protocol. Eye-contact, smile, talk (say something you fool), exchange contact info, make a date, reach out and touch someone, kisses, etc. See how easy it is.

 Love is in the Air

Excuse me, weren't you at the... art exhibit yesterday?
Promiňte, nebyl jste včera na umělecké výstavě?

Let's exchange e-mail addresses/phone numbers.
Vyměňme si e-mailové adresy / telefonní čísla.

What's the matter? **Co se děje?**
Nothing. **nic**

I only have safe sex. **Já mám jenom bezpečný sex.**

How does this feel? **Jak se citiš?**
That feels great. **Je to skvělé.**

I've got some great wine, music,..at my place.
Mám skvělé víno, hudbu… u mě doma.

Hello, could I speak to… **Ahoj, mohu mluvit s…**
I look forward to seeing you. **Těším se, až Vás uvidím.**
Would you like to go out tonight/this Friday for…? **Chtěl bys jít dnes večer/tento pátek ven na…?** a walk, dinner, drink -**procházku, večeři, drink**
Do you want to dance? **Chceš tančit?**
Let's get something to drink. **Dejme si něco k pití.**
Sorry I'm late, there was a a lot of traffic, the metro/tram was late. Please forgive me. **Promiňte že jdu pozdě, byla hustá doprava, metro / tramvaj měla zpoždění. Prosím, odpusťte mi.** My darling, my love, my little beetle, **můj miláčku, moje lásko, můj broučku.**

The World at Large

Do you believe in... astrology, God, UFO's, life after death-
Věříte... astrologii, v Boha, na ufo, v posmrtný život?

I don't believe in.... I'm not sure....
-Nevěřím...Nejsem si jistý...
In the past- **v minulosti**

What do you think about the new..,
-Co si myslíte o....tom novém...

They need to improve...**Musí zlepšit...**

They need to raise/lower... **Musí zvýšit/snížit**
That's a good point.-**To je dobrý postřeh.**

The problem is - **Problém je**
That's true but on the other hand.-
To je pravda, ale na druhou stranu

I feel the same - **Cítím se to stejně**

The solution is - **Řešením je...**
It's a waste of money - **Je to plýtvání peněz**

politics - politika
government - vláda
politicians - politici
liberals - liberálové
conservatives - konzervativci
globalization - globalizace
crime - zločin
mafia - mafie
faith/belief - víra
religion - náboženství
believe - věřit
war - válka

outer space - vesmír
the universe - vesmír
science - věda
economy - ekonomika
violence - násilí
peace - mír
environment - prostředí
global warming -
globální oteplování

Sentence Openers & Other Versatile Phrases

I don't know - nevím...
I didn't know - nevěděl jsem
I know - Já vím...
Do you know...? - Víš/víte...?

I have no idea if...nemám tušení jestli...

Do you think - myslíš...?
I don't think - nemyslím...
I think that - myslím, že ...
I thought - myslel jsem
I thought that - myslel/a jsem, že...

Do you want- chceš
I want - chci
I don't want - nechci
I would like - chtěl bych
Would you like - chtěl bys
I'd rather not - raději bych ne
I would prefer - dal bych přednost
I hope that..- doufám, že..
I wish - přeji si

I said - řekl/a jsem
he said - řekl
he told me - řekl mi

I don't understand - nerozumím

I believe that - věřím, že

Don't worry - neboj se

I believe that - věřím, že

I wonder if - jsem zvědavý, jestli

I like - mám rád
I don't like - nemám rád
I like it very much - mám to velmi rád

I promise - slibuju, že

I saw - viděl/a jsem

I read that - četl/a jsem, že

I heard that - slyšel/a jsem, že

I forgot - zapomněl/a jsem

in case - v případě /in that case - v tom případě

nothing special/much - nic moc

same here - mně taky
you too - ty taky
me too - já taky

How do you say pen in Czech? - Jak se řekne český pen?

Repeat that, please - Opakujte to, prosím.

speak slowly, please - mluvte pomalu, prosím.

How was it? - jak to dopadlo?

Really! Opravdu? Is that a fact? - To je fakt? Seriously - vážně

Certainly - určitě, /sure-jistě
Of course - samozřejmě

it's one and the same/either way/it makes no difference/it doesn't matter - to je jedno

Could you show me that.. - Mohl byste mi ukázat?

a huh - no

bon appetit - dobrou chuť

More Sentence Openers & Other Versatile Phrases

cheers/salute - na zdraví

Excuse me - pardon, promiňte

sorry - sory or promiň
I apologize - omlouvám se

my sympathies - to je mi líto
mrzí mě to

You're welcome/Don't mention it - neni zač/ to nic

It doesn't matter - to nevadí

wait a minute - moment

have a nice day - hezký den

It depends on - to záleží na
then, as in, in that case, or consequently - tedy

then - at that time-tehdy

then-next, after that - potom, po, pak

actually - vlastně

Are you alright? - jste v pořádku?
What happened? - Co se stalo?
Is everything alright? - Je všechno v pořadku
What's the matter? - Co se děje?

you're right - máš pravdu
that's right - to je pravda

that's it - to je ono
like that - takhle

that's an error - to je omyl
that's a mistake/ there is a mistake - to je chyba

It's a joke - to je vtip

that's too bad/what a shame/pity - to je škoda

that's funny - to je legrační

that/it's great - to je prima

By the way - mimochodem

Learning on the Right Side of the Brain

If you are at all familiar with the notion that the brain is divided into right and left hemispheres and that some tasks and activities are favored by one side or the other, you know that artistic type activities take place on the right side of the brain while calculation and active cognition take place on the left. I believe language learning is primarily a right brain activity or perhaps a hybrid between the hemispheres. Traditional language learning approaches lean towards the left brain, which is why they also tend to not be very effective at learning a foreign language.

Real-Time Listening and Speaking Practice

Sections 1 and 2 of Speak Czech Badly represent more of a right or hybrid learning approach whereas Section 3, more of a left brain task. It's my attempt to explain Czech grammar which, when understood, provides a satisfaction to the left brain but does not really enable the actual use of the knowledge learned in real time language ability. For that, you will need "Real-Time" language practice listening and responding to Czech speakers.

Gold Medal Czech Section III

The goal of Speak Czech Badly is the ability to quickly create novel and useful statements, a true step towards language fluency. So far, we have not been overly concerned with grammatical correctness, while at the same time maintaining a level correct enough to be comprehensible. This orientation has allowed us to have a rich foreign language experience and to say more in less time than would be possible using any other approach.

Hopefully, you've been to the Czech Republic on holiday and had a ball or maybe you've been living and working there and getting by using "Bad Czech." Congratulations! You've experienced the thrill of communicating in a foreign language.

But the day may come when you want to go for the Gold medal in the Czech Language. For that, you will need to explore the inner workings of Czech grammar, which will also make possible the addition of a few more expressions to our conversational repertoire.

However, read this section at your own risk. Because once you enter the labyrinth of Czech grammar, you will glimpse what may have shaped the disturbing world of which Franz Kafka wrote.

(By now you should have noticed that apart from the ř and r, pronouncing written Czech words is not that difficult. The previous two sections of the book focused on pronunciation and right brain language skills whereas this section focuses on left brain language know how.)

Inside Czech Grammar

We have travelled quite far and said a great deal without exploring the inner workings of our Czech language engine. However, to go that extra mile and make the last part of our journey possible, we need to add some "high performance" grammatical ingredients to our language fuel mixture.

All About Cases

Do you remember pig Latin, the "secret language" we played with as kids, where you move the first letter to the end of a word and add *ay* to the ends of some words? If I remember right, it goes something like this: The ogday is inay the ardengay eatingay your steakay. (The dog is in the garden eating your steak, for those of you who don't speak pig latin. Well, my version of pig latin)

Czech, along with several other languages, adds endings like these and others to many of their words. If *dog* were a Czech word it would make several more changes that look like this:

singular: dog—doga—dogovi—doga—doge—dogovi—dogem
plural: dogs— dogi—dogu—dogům—dogy—dogi—dogech—dogy

Although some of the endings repeat, there are seven situations or *cases* that require the word dog to change form in the singular as well as the plural. This is true of most Czech nouns and adjectives,(including possessives pronouns like my, your, etc.!).

As this concept is quite foreign to English speakers, we will take this in steps so as to make the process as clear and painless as possible.

Nouns are Sexy in Czech

Before we can talk about nouns like, dogs and cats, mice and men, Paris and Rome or politics and pantyhose, we need to first place these words into gender categories. Categorizing nouns is the first step on the road to making case changes.

Many languages, including Czech, assign a sex or gender to the nouns of their language and label the categories accordingly. So, before we can make case changes, we first need to know to which category the noun we want to change belongs, because each category has its own case ending pattern. The nouns for instance, are classified as being either masculine, feminine, or neuter, (and some languages, like Czech, even have subdivisions within each category). How the words ended up in each category defies logic. However, sometimes it makes sense. The word man, for instance, belongs to the masculine category and the word woman to the feminine. I would consider a chair to be somewhat sexually neuter (with the exception of my vibrating lazy boy) but it is designated as being feminine in Czech (maybe that explains it).

Hold Onto Your Seat

Our Czech grammar life would be relatively simple if there were only three gender categories, but hold onto your seat, there are actually fourteen categories of nouns, you heard me right, fourteen! —six categories of masculine nouns, four feminine and four neuter categories. Since there is no accurate way of guessing a noun's category based on its sexual characteristics, it is best to view the gender categories as nothing more than labels for the categories. Perhaps over a thousand years ago, the originators of this system would have been able to tell us why each noun fits into a particular category, but that knowledge has long since been lost. Now we must rely on other methods for placing the nouns into the correct category, which we will learn shortly.

The real Czech word for dog is *pes* and it belongs to the first category of masculine nouns, labelled mha, which stands for masculine hard animate. The nouns in this category are or were at one time animate, that is, living. Unlike a table, for instance, which is inanimate. However, there are exceptions to this logic, so don't get too focused on the reasoning and simply use the charts which follow to determine the gender of the noun.

Seven ways to say dog in the singular. (woof!)

singular dog	plural dogs
1. pes	psi
2. psa	psů
3. psovi	psům
4. psa	psy
5. pse	psi
6. psovi	psech
7. psem	psy

Regardless of the form that the word pes changes to, we are still talking about the same dog. The various forms however, provide additional grammatical/semantic information in regards to the dog. For instance, if a Czech speaker were to see the word pesem (the seventh case form) in isolation, they would know that someone or something was with the dog.

The following charts are a modified version of what Czech school children use to help them learn the transformation of nouns, known as declensions, in each of the seven cases, in the singular, for all the various masculine, feminine and neuter nouns and their subcategories.

Masculine noun samples

gentleman	castle	man
case MHA	MHI	MSA
singular	singular	singular
1st pán	hrad	muž
2nd pána	hradu	muže
3rd pánovi	hradu	muži
4th pána	hrad	muže
5th pane	— —	muži
6th pánovi	hradu	mužovi, (muži)
7th pánem	hradem	mužem

machine	charman	judge
MSI	MEA	MEE
singular	singular	singular
1st stroj	předseda	soudce
2nd stroje	předsedy	soudce
3rd stroji	předsedovi	soudci
4th stroj	předsedu	soudce
5th — stroji	předsedo	soudce
6th stroji	předsedovi	soudovi, (soudci)
7th strojem	předsedou	soudcem

Feminine noun samples

woman	rose
case FEA	FEE
singular	singular
1st žena	růže
2nd ženy	růže
3rd ženě	růži
4th ženu	růži
5th ženo	růže!
6th ženě	růži
7th ženou	růží

song	bone
FS	FH
singular	singular
píseň	kost
písně	kosti
písni	kosti
píseň	kost
písni	— —
písni	kosti
písní	kostí

Neuter Noun samples

city	sea
case NEO	NEE
singular	singular
1st město	moře
2nd města	moře
3rd městu	moři
4th město	moře
5th — —	— —
6th městě,u	moři
7th městem	mořem

chicken	building
NME	NEI
singular	singular
kuře	stavení
kuřete	stavení
kuřeti	stavení
kuře	stavení
kuře	— —
kuřeti	stavení
kuřetem	stavením

The most difficult part to this language operation is not learning the endings, which can easily be found in the handy charts provided here and elsewhere, but *when* to make these changes.

So, before we learn the rules for making the endings, let's look at some reasons that require the word dog to change to each of these forms.

When to make case ending changes

1st case: The dog is black.
2nd case: The dog's bone is white.
3rd case: He gave a bone to the dog.
4th case: He pet the dog.
5th case: "Here doggy!"
6th case: The bone is in the dog
7th case: He was walking with a dog.

1. The **pes** is black.
2. The bone of the **psa** is white.
3. He gave a bone to the **psovi.**
4. He pet the **psa**
5. "Here **pse!**"
6. The bone is in the **psovi**.
7. He was walking with a **psem.**

You learned, in the brief grammar introduction in Section I, that sentences are created with the parts of speech. These parts work together to create meaning. At minimum, most sentences must contain a noun and a verb, as in "Tom studies". Tom is the noun and studies is the verb. Tom is considered the actor or subject of the sentence. Other sentences also include the recipient of the action of the verb, otherwise known as the object., as in, Tom teaches Susan. Tom is the actor or subject, teaching is the action, and Sue is that which is acted upon, or the object. Czech recognizes these and other relationships between the elements in our sentences and makes word changes to show these relationships.

1st case: The dictionary form of a word is our starting point, which is also the first case form. In the first sentence, the dog is the subject of the verb. You can ask the question, What is black? answer, the dog. So, when a word is the subject of the sentence we will keep that word in it's dictionary and first case form. (grammatically known as the Nominative case)

2nd case: In the second sentence, You could say that the dog is the owner of the bone. So anytime we would say Tom's pen, or the dog's bone or the bone of the dog, the owner, or the thing to which something belongs, will be put in the second case or possessive form (grammatically known as the Genitive case)

4th case: Let's look at the fourth case before looking at the third, which will make it easier to understand the third case. If we ask the question, "Who pet the dog?" the answer is, He did, so now we know the subject. To discover the object we need to ask, What did he pet?, answer, the dog. Which makes dog the object of the verb. Objects of verbs are put in the fourth case (known as the Accusative case)

3rd case: In English, there are certain verbs that allow us to word a sentence in one of two ways with no change in meaning. For instance, in sentence three we could also say "He gave the dog a bone." We can ask the question, What did he give? a dog or a bone? answer, a bone. So bone is the object, which leaves dog, known in English as the indirect object. Indirect objects are changed to the third case form (known as the Dative case)

5th case: My name is Bill but when Czechs call out to me they say "Bille," because Czech makes a case change when calling out to people or dogs, or anything that can be called out to. This one is the simplest to grasp and use. (known as the Vocative or the "calling out" case) It just occurred to me that in English we actually use a calling case in some situations—consider the example, "Here doggy." Dog changes to doggy. Just an amusing thought but it may help explain the calling case a bit. (Although it is possible to call out to inanimate objects in a poetic sense, the declension is not shown in the charts.)

6th case: The sixth case is used with prepositions when showing the location of something with the use of words like on, at, in, over, near and also when using the word *about*. For instance, if you say, "I am in the park," the word park would be put into the seventh case form because it is what the *in* is referring to.(known as the Locative case, as in location)

7th case: This case is used when the means or instrument for carrying out the action is mentioned in the sentence. When you are doing something with something as in,"I am writing with a pen," or going by car, or you are with someone or going with someone, then whatever the with or by is referring to will be in the 7th case. (known as the Instrumental case, as in the means by which something is done.)

Later we will learn additional reasons for making case changes, but for now let's learn how to determine a noun's category.

How to determine a noun's category

The best way to determine a noun's category is to first determine its major gender by using a Czech/English dictionary which shows gender, because not all do. There will be an abbreviation such as Ma, Mi, F, N after the Czech word. Ma stands for masculine animate, Mi for masculine inanimate, F is for female and N for neuter. Of the fourteen categories, these are the major ones and most nouns fit into them. Unfortunately, the dictionaries do not show the subcategories. Though, once we know these broad categories, we can, with the help of the Last Letter Brain on page 142, determine which of the subcategories our noun belongs to.

Without a dictionary it is possible to determine gender with about an 80% accuracy. For instance:

Most masculine nouns end in consonants
Most feminine nouns end in the letter a
Most neuter nouns end in the letter o

Gender jump-start

In the word list included in the vocabulary section at the end of this book, the gender of the noun and its category have been included to allow you to put them to use as quickly as possible.

Once you know which category the noun belongs to, you will turn to the Noun Transformation Brain on the following page which shows all fourteen categories and the endings that go with each category. The mini chart on the next page is an excerpt which was used to create the endings for pes. Let's see how this was done.

Now that we know that the word pes belongs to the MHA category we can make the transformations (technically known as declensions)

Look at the mini sample chart on the next page. It shows the endings for the nouns that belong in the MHA category both in the singular and plural.

How to make the case ending changes

Now let's learn how to make the case endings.

Look at number one under the singular heading in the chart in the chart below. You will see the word base. Here you will place the Czech noun as it appears in the dictionary. So pes is our starting point and the form we would use in sentences when dog is the subject.

1st case the base word is the dictionary form of the word, pán
2nd case (+a means to add the letter a to the end of
the base word) so we add an *a* to pán and get pána
3rd case (+ovi means to add ovi to the base word-pánovi)
4th case (+a means to add the letter a, just like the 2nd case-pána)
5th case (+e means to add the letter e-pane)
6th case (+ovi is like the 3rd case- pánovi)
7th case (+em means to add the letters em- pánem)

MHA		gentleman	
singular		case	MHA
		singular	
1.	base	1st	pán
2.	+a	2nd	pána
3.	+ovi	3rd	pánovi
4.	+a	4th	pána
5.	+e	5th	pane
6.	+ovi	6th	pánovi
7.	+em	7th	pánem

Now turn the page and view the charts for all fourteen categories. Note that some categories show a minus and plus sign. This means to first remove the last letter from the base word and then add the letter or letters shown there. For example, look at the FEA category, which stands for feminine nouns ending in the letter a. Look at the second case which has -+ y. Let's use the most feminine of all feminine words—woman, which in Czech is žena. The instructions say to remove the last letter and add y, which creates ženy—the second case form of žena.

Some categories show an equal sign, which means the word in that case is the same as the base word, in other words, no changes are made. Others show −2+, which means to remove the last two letters from the base word and then add the letter or letters shown. And finally, in the fifth case you will often see this --- sign which means the word isn't used in that case. Being the case where you call out to someone, it makes sense that you wouldn't call out to a tree for instance. So, it is not applicable.

Noun Brain
Chart Abbreviations
Masculine Noun Headings

MHA (masculine hard animate) end in hard consonants
MHI (masculine hard inanimate)
MSA (masculine soft animate)
MSI (masculine soft inanimate)
MEA (masculine nouns ending in a)
MEE (masculine nouns ending in e)

Female Noun Headings

FEA (feminine ending a)
FEE (feminine ending e)
FS (feminine soft)
FH (feminine hard)

Neuter Noun Headings

NEO (neuter ending o)
NEE (neuter ending e)
NME (neuter mixed ending)
NEI (neuter ending I)

Base is the dictionary form of word
+ means to add the letter shown to the end of the base word.
-+means to remove the last letter from the base word and add the letter(s) shown.
-2+ means to remove the last two letters from the base word and add the letter(s) shown.
— means that no form exists
= form is the same as base word

Masculine Noun Categories

case MHA		MHI	
singular	plural	singular	plural
1st base	+i	base	+y
2nd +a	+ů	+u	+ů
3rd +ovi/u	+ům	+u	+ům
4th +a	+y	=	+y
5th +e	+i	—	—
6th +ovi/u	+ech	+u	+ech
7th +em	+y	+em	+y

MSA		MSI	
singular	plural	singular	plural
base	+i/ové	base	+e
+e	+ů	+e	+ů
+i/ovi	+ům	+i	+ům
+e	+e	=	+e
+i	+i/ové	—	—
+i/ovi	+ích	+i	+ích
+em	+i	+em	+í

MEA		MEE	
singular	plural	singular	plural
base	-+ ové	base	-+i/ové
-+ y	-+ů	=	-+ů
-+ ovi	-+ům	-+ i /ovi	-+ům
-+ u	-+y	=	=
-+ o	-+ové	=	=/ové
-+ ovi	-+ech	-+i/ovi	-+ích
-+ ou	-+y	-+ em	-+i

The column to the right is an exceptional case of MHI nouns in the singular which have their own endings as shown. Nouns in this category include months and days.

MHI
singular
base
+a
+u
=
—
+u
+em

Female Noun Categories

case	FEA		FEE	
	singular	plural	singular	plural
1st	base	-+y	base	=
2nd	-+ y	-a	=	-+í
3rd	-+ ě	-+ám	-+ i	-+ím
4th	-+ u	-+y	-+ i	=
5th	-+ o	-+y	—	—
6th	-+ ě	-+ách	-+ i	-+ích
7th	-+ ou	-+mi	-+í	+mi

FS		FH	
singular	plural	singular	plural
base	-2+ně	base	+i
-2+ně	-2+ní	+ i	+í
-2+ni	-2+ním	+ i	+em
=	-2+ně	=	+í
—	—	—	—
-2+ni	-2+ních	+ i	+ech
-2+ní	-2+němi	+ í	+mi

Neuter Noun Categories

case	NEO		NEE	
singular	plural	singular	plural
1st base	-+a	base	=
2nd -+ a	-a	2nd =	-+í
3rd -+ u	-+ům	3rd -+ i	-+ím
4th =	-+a	4th =	=
5th —	—	5th —	—
6th -+ ě	-+ech	6th -+ i	-+ích
7th -+ em	-+y	7th +m	-+i

NME		NEI	
singular	plural	singular	plural
base	-+ata	base	=
-+ te	-+at	=	=
-+ ti	-+atům	=	+m
=	-+ata	=	=
=	-+ata	—	—
-+ ti	-+atech	=	+ch
+ tem	-+aty	+ m	+mi

Exceptions

No Czech grammar point would be complete without mentioning the exceptions to the rule. You may have noticed that the word *dog - pes*, does not become *pesa* in the second case but instead changes to *psa*. Although it does end in the letter *a* as the rules states, the letter *e* is removed. Several Czech words change spelling in other ways and there is no rule which covers all situations in which they do so. Some categories with exceptional spelling changes include the days of the week, months, proper names, among others. Exceptions can only be learned as you encounter them, unfortunately.

How to determine sub-categories

Suppose you need to use a word not included on the vocabulary list in this book.

Step 1. Go to an English/Czech dictionary or ask a Czech person and find out if the noun is masculine, feminine, or neuter. If you've been following along you might be asking how you further categorize a noun into one of the sub-categories?

For this, you need to learn how the Czech consonants themselves are classified.

Consonants are classified into three groups. The names given to these groups are hard, soft and neutral.

> ## The Last Letter Brain
> Hard include the letters: h,ch,k,r,d,t,n,g
> Soft include: š,č,ř,ž,c,j,d',t',n'
> neutral: b,f,l,m,p,s,v,z

Once we know the broad category of masculine, feminine or neuter, we can determine the sub-category based on the last letter of the word in its dictionary or first case form, and if masculine, whether or not the noun in question was ever living, that is, animate.

Let's try one. Suppose the word you want to categorize is bone. You find out that the Czech word for bone is kost and that it is a feminine noun. Kost ends in the letter t. We then go to the Last Letter Brain and find that the letter t is in the Hard group. You then go to the feminine category in the noun brain and hope there is a category labeled feminine hard or (FH) for short. Hurray, there is, which places the word kost into the FH (feminine hard) category.

Some masculine nouns end in the letter *a* and we just learned that some feminine nouns end in consonants. However, only a small percentage do. Most words that end in consonants are masculine and most that end in the letter *a* are feminine and all letters that end in *o* are neuter. So, if you were to just guess based on this knowledge you would do alright. In fact, in the vocabulary list included in this book, 99% of the words ending in *a* are feminine and 91% of the words ending in consonants are masculine.

How to create plurals

Once we know the dictionary base word and the category the noun belongs to, we can simply follow the instructions for creating regular plurals in the Noun Transformation Brain.

For example: Place the word *kost* into the FH category. Here, the instruction for creating the plural in the first case is +i which creates kosti (bones).

Worth noting, is that in general, most nouns are either masculine inanimate nouns or feminine nouns ending in a. Both of these groups form the plural with a y ending. Thus, žena becomes ženy (women) and *most* (bridge) becomes *mosty* (bridges). Also, most neuter nouns end in o and form their plural in the first case by removing the o and replacing it with the letter a, thus pivo (beer) becomes piva (beers). It is easy to become mislead by a word you see with an *a* ending and believe it to be a feminine word but in actuality it is a plural neuter word. Of course, the word changes form in all the other cases, with a great deal of repetition, fortunately.

Irregular Plurals

In English, we create the plural by adding the letter s to most nouns, ie., bone-bones. However, we do have several exceptions to this rule. Consider how man becomes men in the plural, child to children. And some words don't change at all—one sheep, two sheep, etc..

Czech also has several irregular plural formations. Here are some of the most common irregular forms that don't follow the rules for making plurals given in the Noun Transformation Brain.

1. Nouns that end in soft consonants (see the Last Letter Brain) usually add an e to form the nominative plural: klíč (key) becomes klíče (keys).
2. Nouns that end in consonants preceded by an e as in pes (dog) tend to move the e to the end of the word or remove the e and then add a y ending. For example: pes becomes psi (dogs) in the plural, koberec (rug) becomes koberce (rugs), broskev (peach) becomes broskve (pears), den (day) becomes dny (days), dárek gift becomes dárky gifts.
3. Others involve vowel changes as in kůň (horse) becoming koně (horses), dům (home) becomes domy (homes), stůl (table) becomes stoly (tables).

There are others and there are rules for forming these irregulars but there are exceptions in almost in every category. These irregular plurals are best learned one at a time as you encounter them. But one last one you should know before leaving the subject of irregular plurals is dítě (child) which becomes děti children.

Declining Irregular Nouns

Once you learn the irregular form of the noun (best to ask a Czech speaker) you can use the rules as shown in the Noun Transformation Brain for declining the noun in each case.

Other Reasons for Making Case Changes

Here are some additional reasons that require nouns to change form in each of the seven cases.

1. Nominative case: When a noun is the subject of the sentence, it will remain in its dictionary base form. In some sentences however, it is not always clear what the subject is.

a. In questions: Where are the keys? Kde jsou klíče? (keys is the subject)
b. with pronouns: This is a new book. (This is the subject, but this is referring to the book, so book is in the first or nominative case.

2. Genitive case: The genitive case shows that to which something belongs. As in:

a. Bill's car. The name Bill, being masculine will change form according to the gender of the noun which follows. The word car is a neuter noun in Czech, so Bill would change to Billovo auto. In Czech, you would in affect be saying, the car of Bill.
b. a map of China: China would be put into its gentive form.
c. the genitive case is used after most quantifiers, such as, a little (trochu) very (moc), a lot (hodně, small (málo), and others
d. after some prepositions, in particular, without (bez)
e. after some verbs like, to fear - bát se or to avoid - vyvarovat se
f. and as we will learn later it is used with dates and time

3. Dative case: We learned that after certain verbs indirect objects can be included in our sentences thus requiring the use of the dative case in Czech. The dative case is sometimes referred to as "the giving case" because many of the verbs used here tend to imply the transfer of something from one person or thing to another. Not surprisingly, some common verbs used like this include:

to give-dávat	He gave a pen to me.
to send-posílat	He sent a fax to me.
to say/tell-říkat	He told me the news.
to thank-děkovat	He thanked me for the gift.

In English, we can usually word these sentences in two ways with no change in meaning. For example, "He sent me a fax", could replace the example above. Czech puts the direct object after the verb as in the examples above.

b. after some prepositions: nouns following these prepositions and others are put into the dative case.

towards, in the direction of	**k;ke**
opposite	**naproti**
on account of	**kvůli**

4. Accusative case: As mentioned earlier, the direct object of the sentence is put into the accusative form.

a. Also after some prepositions:
on, for-	**na**
for-	**pro**

Ex: I am going for coffee.
Jdu na kávu. (kavu /coffee is in its accusative form.

It is a present for you.
To je dárek pro tebe. (tebe is the accusative form of *you*)

5. Vocative case: People's names change form to show that you are calling out to them. The main rules for these changes include the following: The rules apply mainly to animate nouns since only living things like people and animals are normally called out to.

a. Add the letter *e* to male names ending in hard consonants, such as Jakub, which becomes Jakube! Others move the e such as Karel becoming Karle! Other names that end in consonants, with the exception of those mentioned below also add an e ending, thus Bill becomes Bille.
b. names ending in *k, h,* or *ch* add the letter *u*. Thus Vojtěch becomes Vojtěchu!
c. names ending in *ek* like Marek become Marku!
d. names ending in soft consonants like Luboš add an *i* and become Luboši!
e. some names like Jiří stay the same
f. names that end in an *r* preceeded by a consonant change to *ře* as in Petr becoming Petře.
g. Women's names ending in *a*, as most do, change the *a* to an *o*, as Jana becoming Jano! (men's names ending in *a* also change to *o*)
h. names ending in *ie,* like Lucie stay the same.

6. Locative case: The nouns following some prepositions that show where something is located are changed to the sixth case or locative form. (Other prepositions which show other locations take the instrumental case, see next number) For example: The book is in the library. The word *in* is the preposition in this sentence and the word library changes form to agree with this preposition. The following prepositions require the nouns which follow to be in their locative case form.

a. in or at - **v/ve** (v and ve have the same meaning, ve is used in front of some words to aid pronunciation.

b. on or at					**na**

c. These prepositions express		**po, přes**
being somewhere and moving
somewhere at the same time,
as in, I was running *through* the park
or walking *on* or *through* the streets or *over* the bridge.

d. about: the locative case is used	**o**
when combining the preposition
about with some verbs, as in,
They were talking *about* you.

7. Instrumental case: The instrumental case is used when discussing the means by which something is done. As in, I write with a pencil, or I am going there by car. It is used after the preposition *with* and the following:

with	**s/se** (remember, se has other uses, pg. 75)
in front of	**před**
above	**nad**
under	**pod**
between	**mezi**

There are other reasons for making case changes not mentioned here but to include more now would only serve to overwhelm and not instruct. And you really shouldn't expect to put even the ones mentioned here into use without some sort of intensive and focused practice. If you become more immersed in the language you will learn more as needed, through experience and exposure to the language.

More Help for Determining Case Endings

You can use these sentences as models for determining which case to use for the words in your own sentences. The number at the end of the sentence indicates the case of noun depending on its grammatical role in that sentence.

Thought Pattern Case Endings

Thought Pattern 1. Things (nouns) and people as subjects
He (1) is a teacher(1). On je učitel. He (1) isn't a teacher(1). On není učitel. Is he (1) a teacher(1)? Je učitel?

Thought Pattern 2. States (adjectives)
He (1) is tired(1).On je unavený. He (1) isn't tired(1). Není unavený. Is he (1) tired (1).? Je unavený.?

Thought Pattern 3. Places (adverbials of time and space)
He (1) is in the library(6). On je v knihovně. He (1) isn't in the library(6). Není v knihovně. Is he (1) in the library(6)? Je v knihovně?

Thought Pattern 4. Activities (verbs)
He(1)is working. On pracuje. He (1) isn't working. Nepracuje. Is he (1) working? Pracuje?

Thought Pattern 5. People and things as objects
She(1) is waiting for me(4). Čeká na mě.

Thought Pattern 6. Possessions
Her pen(1) is on the table(6). Její pero je na stole. Bob's pen(1) is on the table (6). Bobovo pero je na stole. This is a map(1) of China(2). To je mapaČíny.

Thought Pattern 7. Qualitites (more adjectives)
The pen(1) is red(1). To pero je červené. The red(1) pen(1) is better than the green(1) pen(1). To červené pero je lepší než to zelené pero. The blue(1) pen(1) is best. To modré pero je nejlepší.

Thought Pattern 8. This/That- This pen (1) is red (1). Toto pero je červené. This is a red (1) pen (1). Toto je červené pero.

Thought Pattern 9. Positions/Directions/Relationships (prepositions)
Meet me in the library(6)/in the park(6)/at the store(6). Sejdeme se v knihovně./v parku/v obchodě. The pen(1) is in the drawer(6)/ on the table(6)/under the book(7). To pero je v šuplíku/na stole/pod knihou(7). This book(1) is about dogs(6). Tato kniha je o psech. This book(1) is for you(4). Tato kniha je pro vás.

Thought Pattern 10. Info Questions
Who is that? Kdo je to? Where is the cinema(1)? Kde je kino? When does the film(1) start? Kdy začíná film? etc.

Thought Pattern 11. Modal Questions (offers, Invitations, Requests,)
Would you like to go to the cinema(2) tonight? Šel bys dnes večer do kina? or Chtěl bys jít dnes večer do kina?

Thought Pattern 12. Establishing Existence
There is a full moon tonight(1). Dnes večer je úplněk. There are pubs in Prague. There are many pubs(2) in Prague(6). V Praze je hodně hospod. It is raining. Prší.

Thought Pattern 13. Judgments and possibilities
We could go to a café(2). Mohli bychom jít do kavárny. We should have stayed home(4). Měli jsme zůstat doma. I would do it like this. Udělal bych to takhle.

Thought Pattern 14. Conditions
If I were you(7),I wouldn't eat that(4), . Kdybych byl tebou(7), tak bych to(4) nejedl.

Thought Pattern 15. Indefinite time/place/people/things—Quantifiers
Has anybody(1) been here? Byl tady někdo? Do you have any English(4) newspapers(4)? Máš nějaké anglické noviny. Do you have any newspapers(4) in English(6)? Máš nějaké noviny v angličtině?

Thought Pattern 16. Connectors - I also like chocolate(4). Mám taky rád čokoládu.

Thought Pattern 17. Related Thoughts (clauses)
She is the woman(1) that(6) I told you(3) about. To je ta žena, o které jsem ti vyprávěl.

Thought Pattern 18. Commands: Call me/Meet me/Wait/Come here. Zavolej/Sejdeme se/Počkej/Pojď sem.

Thought Pattern 19. Unknown actors (passive) My wallet was stolen. Ukradli mi(3) peněženku(4).

Nothing but a great deal of practice and familiarity with the reasons for making case changes will enable you to quickly determine to which case you must change the nouns and pronouns in your statements. At first you will go very slowly as you have to think out your thoughts before you say them.

Try guessing the case of the nouns in the language lab below using the reasons you have learned thus far.

Language Creation Lab # 13

Guess the case of all the nouns in each sentence.

1. The pen is on the table.
2. She sent a fax.
3. They talked about the weather.

Upside-down solution

Lab #13

1. The pen is on the table.= Pero je na stole. (The word pen is in the first case and table is in the sixth case.)
2. She sent a fax. = Poslala fax. (The word she is in the first case and fax is in the fourth case.)
3. They talked about the weather.= Mluvili o počasí. (The word they is in the first case and weather is in the sixth case.

This/That/These/Those Revisited

Although the Czech language does not use articles like *a, an* and *the*, per se, it does have an elaborate and profuse system for identifying, pointing out and distinguishing one item from another.

English has only the words *this, that, these* and *those*, grammatically known as demonstrative pronouns or demonstrative adjectives depending how they are used in a sentence.

In the "Bad Czech" section, we learned the oversimplified versions for this, that, these and those, *to* for this, *to* or *tamto* for that, *tyto* for these and *tamty* for those. Here we will look at the ugly grammatical truth for using these "pointer" words correctly in Czech.

In English, *this* and *that* are used to distinguish between things which may be near or away from the speaker or to distinguish one item from another. The word *the* can also be used to distinguish one item from another as in, " *The* man at the door is my brother.," as opposed to the man at the window.

Consider the difference between sentence 1 and 2 below:

1. That is an old book. To/Tohle/toto je stará kniha.
2. That book is old. Ta/Tato/tahle kniha je stará.

In sentence 1, *that* is being used as a pronoun and in sentence 2 as an adjective.

Notice the various Czech forms which can be used. Czech has formal and informal variations of these words and as in English even "country" variations, as in "this here book", or "this one here." A chart for these "pointer" words appears on the next page and in the Appendix you will be mesmerized by the myriad forms and their formal and informal use.

When used as a pronoun in Czech, as in sentence 1 above, you can use the word *to* in all situations and whether or not you are referring to one or more items, that is, singular or plural. Notice that *to* is used in both of the sentences below, where English notes the difference in singular and plural by using *that* or *those*.

a. That is an old book.   To je stará kniha.
b. Those are old books.   To jsou staré knihy.

However, when these pronouns act as adjectives they change form according to gender and case which we will look at shortly. Before we look at these forms, let's first make a few more general observations for their use in sentences. Also as mentioned earlier, English, at times, uses the word *the* to point things out where it can often be interchanged with *that* or *this* with no change in meaning and at times, the word *it* can be substituted for *this* or *that* as well.

Consider the following sentences:

a. (There is) A book is on the table.   Kniha je na stole.
literally: Book is on table.

In this simple sentence, which English can begin with *There is* or *A,* nothing is used before the words book and table in Czech because Czech doesn't use articles to mark nouns and because there is no need to distinguish between two items in the sentence above.

b. A man is at the door.   U dveří je nějaký muž.

Czech word order often begins the sentence with the prepositional or adverbial phrase. So this sentence reads, At the door is *some* man. Czech often uses the word some/*nějaký* which we do sometimes in English as well. We could say, "Some man is at the door." More on word order and how *nějaký* changes form later.

c. The book is old.   Kniha je stará.

Nothing is being pointed at or out or distinguished, so no word is used before the word book-kniha.

d. The/that book on the table is old.   Ta kniha na stole je stará.

In sentence d, there is more of a sense of something being pointed out, so the demonstrative adjective *ta* is used. It is joined with the word book/*kniha,* which is feminine and in the first case. Notice that nothing is used before *table* where English uses the word *the*, because we are not distinguishing the table in any way.

As mentioned earlier, demonstrative adjectives follow the gender of the noun they are referring to, so they come in three genders in each of the cases.

First case singular
Masculine	ten	ten sýr	(that cheese)
Feminine	ta	ta kniha	(that book)
Neuter	to	to pivo	(that beer)

Now look at the demonstrative adjective chart next page.

Notice that *ten, ta,* and *to* change in each case, both in the singular and plural.

	the/that/this/these/those for identifying items The film I saw was good. That apple on the table is rotten.							
	Masculine sing.	plural	Masc Inanimate sing.	plural	Feminine sing.	plural	Neuter sing.	plural
1st	ten	ti	ten	ty	ta	ty	to	ta
2nd	toho	těch			té	těch	toho	těch
3rd	tomu	těm			té	těm	tomu	těm
4th	toho	ty	ten	ty	tu	ty	to	ta
6th	o tom	o těch			o té	o těch	o tom	o těch
7th	s tím	s těmi			s tou	s těmi	s tím	s těmi

Examples in each case:

case 1. That boy is small.   **Ten** kluk je malý.
case 2. I'm not going there without that boy. Bez **toho** kluka tam nepůjdu.
case 3. Give it to that boy.   Dej to **tomu** klukovi
case 4. I don't know that boy.   Nevidím **toho** kluka.
case 6. I've never heard of that boy.   **o tom** klukovi jsem nikdy neslyšel
case 7. I'm going to the park with that boy.   Půjdu do parku **s tím** klukem

When used as demonstrative *pronouns* you can use the same pronouns both in the singular and plural: Czech and English are being used in the same sentence to highlight the use of the pronouns.

This is a boy.   To je boy.
That is a boy.   Tamto je boy.
These are boys. To jsou boys.
Those are boys. Tamto jsou boys.

And you can use the same pronouns for feminine and neuter words as well:

This is a girl.   To je girl.
That is a girl.   Tamto je girl..

These are girls. To jsou girls.
Those are girls. Tamto jsou girls.

As mentioned earlier, English makes a distinction between objects that are nearer or farther from the speaker. We say *this* pen, if it is closer to us and *that* pen if it is further or away from us in perspective in time or space. Czech is not as particular about this issue.

In the Appendix, you will see the unbelievable forms of these pointer words. The use of these demonstrative adjectives are dizzying and at times even Czechs violate the grammatical rules in their use. This underscores that language is more of an art than a science.

Fact Czech

Prague's public transportation system is unsurpassed! It's fast and easy to get anywhere! One ticket allows you to hop on and off buses, trams and the metro.

* Lines are constantly being expanded, so by the time this book comes to press, it is likely the end points of these metro lines will be different.

SPEAK CZECH BADLY! BUT SPEAK IT TODAY!

Me again

Now that we are familiar with the concept of cases, and how one word can have seven forms, consider again the *object* pronouns me, you, him, her, it, us, and them. These pronouns also change form according to case.

See the full-sized "Me Brain" on the facing page. Fortunately, the pronouns change cases for the same reason as nouns. Notice that in English we would use the word *him* in all of these sentences. Czech changes the word to clarify the role it is playing in the sentence. If you want to talk about you or me or anybody else, simply substitute these pronouns in each case, ie., She took a picture of me. The word *of* is a clue to use the second case form of *me*.

On page 44, in Section I, a default mini-me brain was created for Bad Czech. You would be understood using that chart alone but this is the full-sized Gold Medal version.

Language Creation Lab #14

For this exercise, simply identify the case of *you* in each sentence.

a. I want to go with you.
b. This book is for you.
c. I sent the message to you yesterday.
d. I'm thinking about you.

(Answers to Lab # 14 on page 162)

---

*As these are object pronouns there is no first case form which are the subject pronouns, I, He, She, etc.

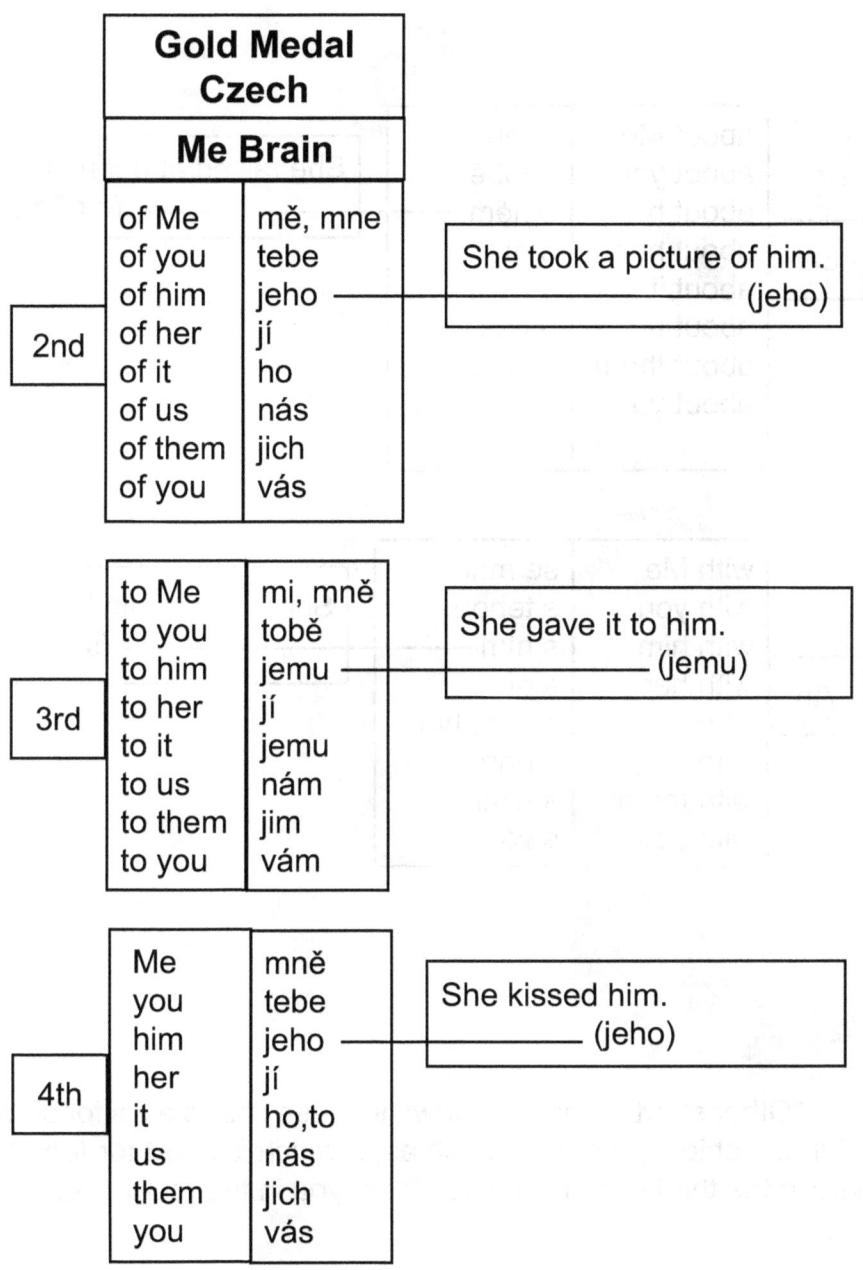

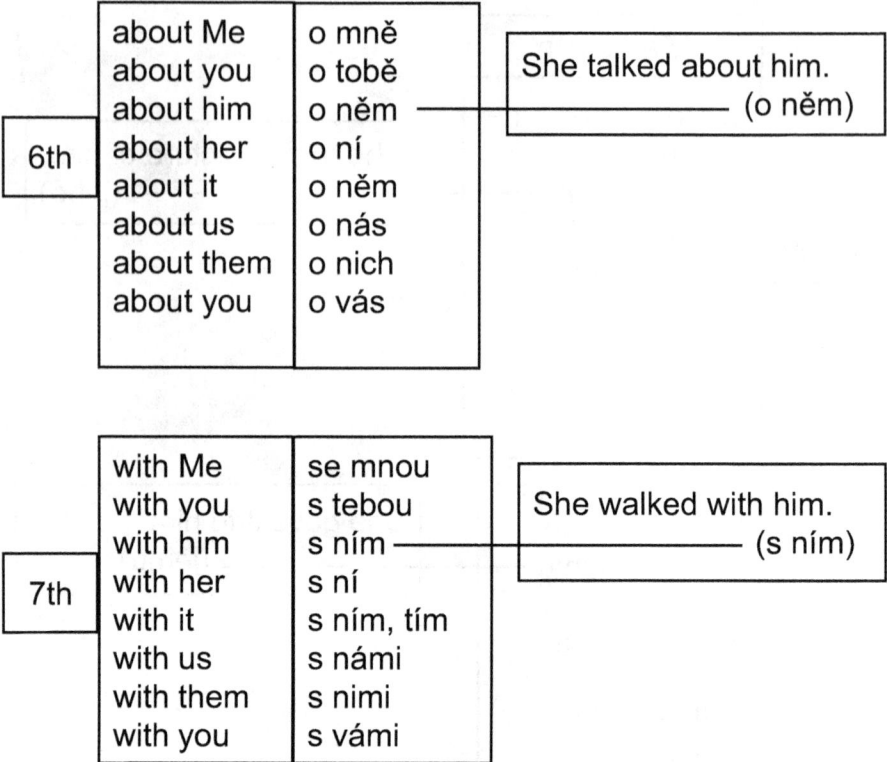

*Other short forms not shown in these charts exist for some of these object pronouns, such as, *ti* which is short for *tobě* for *you* in the third case and *tě* for *tebe, you* in the fourth case.

What about **My** Stuff

Most things in the world belong to somebody, so how do we say, "She pet *my* dog." We can now say *I*, we can now say *me* (in five ways) and we know how to say dog in seven ways (fourteen if you count the plural, so there must be more ways of saying *my*, or *your*, or *his*, *her*, etc..

Turn the page and look at the Gold Medal Possessive Brain. It's not as bad as it looks.

If you look closely, you will see that the word *my* changes in six of the seven cases (no 5th calling case) and that it also changes for each gender of noun, both in the singular and plural for a grand total of thirty-six possible transformations. (fortunately, there is a great deal of repetition) Also fortunate is that they only follow the broad classes of masculine, feminine and neuter—none of the sub-categories.

Here's how it works. The possessive pronouns (*my*, *his*, *your*, etc.) follow the case of the noun in the sentence. For example:

She walked with my dogs = Procházela se s mými psy.

We know that dog is a neuter noun, but this sentence says dogs, so it is in the plural. Find the neuter plural column in the brain. From a previous example, we know that dogs should be in the seventh case in this type of sentence. Go down the column until you come to the seventh case. Here we find that the word *my* should be mými. We know that dogs in the seventh case is psy. So the sentence in Czech should read: "Procházela se s mými psy." If you wanted to say *your* dogs (let's assume it's a friend of yours, so we'll use the informal form of *your*, instead of *my* dogs you would just substitute *your* as it appears in the seventh neuter plural column. Simple. the word is tvými. So, the sentence would read:
"Procházela se s tvými psy."

The Possessive Brain

		Masculine sing. plural		Feminine sing. plural		Neuter sing. plural	
1st	my	můj	mí/mé	má	mé	mé	má
	your	tvůj	tví/tvé	tvá	tvé	tvé	tvá
	his/its	jeho	jeho	jeho	jeho	jeho	jeho
	her	její	její	její	její	její	její
	our	náš	naši/naše	naše	naše	naše	naše
	your	váš	vaši/vaše	vaše	vaše	vaše	vaše
	their	jejich	jejich	jejich	jejich	jejich	jejich
	reflexive	svůj	sví/své	svá	své	své	svá
2nd	my	mého	mých	mé	mých	mého	mých
	your	tvého	tvých	tvé	tvých	tvého	tvých
	his/its	jeho	jeho	jeho	jeho	jeho	jeho
	her	jejího	jejích	její	jejích	jejího	jejích
	our	našeho	našich	naší	našich	našeho	našich
	your	vašeho	vašich	vaší	vašich	vašeho	vašich
	their	jejich	jejich	jejich	jejich	jejich	jejich
	reflexive	svého	svých	své	svých	svého	svých
3rd	my	mému	mým	mé	mým	mému	mým
	your	tvému	tvým	tvé	tvým	tvému	tvým
	his/its	jeho	jeho	jeho	jeho	jeho	jeho
	her	jejímu	jejím	její	jejím	jejímu	její
	our	našemu	našim	naší	našim	našemu	našim
	your	vašemu	vašim	vaší	vašim	vašemu	vašim
	their	jejich	jejich	jejich	jejich	jejich	jejich
	reflexive	svému	svým	své	svým	svému	svým
4th	my	můj	mí/mé	má	mé	mé	má
	your	tvůj	tví/tvé	tvá	tvé	tvé	tvá
	his/its	jeho	jeho	jeho	jeho	jeho	jeho
	her	její	její	její	její	její	její
	our	náš	naši/naše	naše	naše	naše	naše
	your	váš	vaši/vaše	vaše	vaše	vaše	vaše
	their	jejich	jejich	jejich	jejich	jejich	jejich
	reflexive	svůj	sví/své	svá	své	své	svá

The Possessive Brain

	Masculine sing.	Masculine plural	Feminine sing.	Feminine plural	Neuter sing.	Neuter plural
my ⁶ᵗʰ	můj	mí/mé	má	mé	mé	má
your	tvůj	tví/tvé	tvá	tvé	tvé	tvá
his/its	jeho	jeho	jeho	jeho	jeho	jeho
her	její	její	její	její	její	její
our	náš	naši/naše	naše	naše	naše	naše
your	váš	vaši/vaše	vaše	vaše	vaše	vaše
their	jejich	jejich	jejich	jejich	jejich	jejich
reflexive	svůj	sví/své	svá	své	své	svá
my ⁷ᵗʰ	mým	mými	mou	mými	mým	mými
your	tvým	tvými	tvou	tvými	tvým	tvými
his/its	jeho	jeho	jeho	jeho	jeho	jeho
her	její	jejími	její	jejími	její	jejími
our	našim	našimi	naši	našimi	našim	našimi
your	vaším	vašimi	vaší	vašimi	vaším	vašimi
their	jejich	jejich	jejich	jejich	jejich	jejich
reflexive	svým	svými	svou	svými	svým	svými

Let's create some possessive sentences.

Language Creation Lab #15

a) The dog is playing with your children.
b) I fed my dog this morning.
c) My dog is running in your yard.
d) My dog is sleeping in his yard.
e) A blind man would be lost without his dog.
f) She misses her dog.
g) Your dog is big.

(Answers to Lab #15 on page 162)

Reflexive Pronouns
"Peter gave Paul his mobile phone."

In the above statement, do you know whose mobile phone it is? In English, this statement can mean that Peter gave Paul Paul's phone or it can mean that Peter gave Paul Peter's mobile phone. The Czech language has a nifty way of avoiding this ambiguity by using the pronouns listed as reflexive, which you can find below the word *their* in each of the seven cases.

Look at the first case singular Masculine column in the Possessive Brain above. There you will find the word jeho listed for *his*. Jeho would be used in the first example as in "Peter gave Paul jeho phone," as in Paul's phone. Now go down the column to the Reflexive row and find the word svůj, which would be used to show the difference in meaning as in, "Peter gave Paul svůj phone," as in Peter's phone.

Lab #14
Answers
1. I want to go with you.= **Chci jít s tebou.**
2. He left without an umbrella.= **Odešel bez deštníku.**
3. This book is for you.=**Tato kniha je pro tebe.**
4. I sent the message to you yesterday.=
   Včera jsem poslal zprávu.
5. I'm thinking about you.= **Myslím na tebe.**

Lab #15
Answers
1. The dog is playing with our children.= **Pes si hraje s našimi dětmi.**
2. I fed my dog this morning.= **Dnes ráno jsem nakrmil psa.**
3. My dog is running in your yard.= **Můj pes běha ve tvé zahradě.**
4. My dog is sleeping in his yard.= **Můj pes spí v jeho zahradě.**
5. A blind man would be lost without his dog.=
   Slepý muž by byl ztracen bez svého psa.
6. She misses her dog.= **Stýská se jí po jejím psu.**
7. Your dog is big.= **Tvůj pes je velký.**

In Living Color

Now, let's add a little color to our world. What's the Gold Medal way of saying the *big* dog, or *red* wine?

Now that we've mastered how to say *my* or *your* or *his* dog in thirty-six ways, learning how to say the *black* dog or my *black* dogs will be as easy as 1-2-3...45!

We've been adding the number of ways to say the same word, so it should come as no surprise to find that there are forty-five ways to say the word *big* or *red*, or almost any other adjective. Or rather, forty-five grammatical considerations for choosing the correct form of the adjective to use, since many repeat. Adjectives win the prize for the most number of ways to say the same word.

Adjectives follow the gender and number of the noun and the case. For example:

Masculine	Feminine	Neuter
The big man	The big woman	The big beer
The big men	The big women	The big beers

In Czech, each use of *big* in the above examples would use a different form of *big* as follows:

The velký man	The velká woman	The velké beer
The velcí men	The velké women	The velká beers

These are the first case forms. The second case would look like this:

velkého man   velké woman   velkého beer

And so on. Thus, the word big changes in every case as well.

Fortunately, the adjectives follow only the broad categories of masculine animate, feminine and neuter nouns, as well as masculine inanimate nouns, however, most of these are identical to the masculine animate nouns.

See the *Adjective Declension Brain* on the next page. Notice that there are two brains for adjectives because there are two categories of adjectives in Czech. Notice, the endings in brain two are different from the endings in brain one. (Happily, even more repeat here) However, most adjectives are of the "Hard Brain" type. They are called hard and soft because the ý ending is considered a hard letter and the í ending a soft letter. (see the Last Letter Brain pg. 142)

Let's try a couple of examples and let's do them in steps.

1. The dog is on the grass. Pes je na trávě (If we look at the model sentences on page 133, we see that *dog* is in the first case)

2. The Czech word for *black* is černý. It is of the hard type. "The black dog is on the grass." (This sentence is the same as the first one except for the addition of the word black, dog is still in the first case, so black will also be in the first case, dog is a neuter noun and we're talking about one dog, so we go to the neuter singular column in the first case and we find -/+ é. Which means to drop the last letter and add the letter é. So, černý becomes černé. Černý pes je na trávě.

Let's try this one:
1. She pet the dogs. (again, look at the model sentences on page 133 and find the one that most resembles this one.
2. She pet my black dogs. (dogs is still in the fourth case, so black will be in the fourth case as will the word my) They all follow the case of the word dogs in this sentence. Pohladila moje černé psy.

Now, look at Adjective Brain #2.

The vocabulary brain at the back of the book includes about a hundred of the most useful adjectives and shows which adjective brain each adjective belongs to for most of the adjectives there. The remainder you will learn to do on your own.

The procedure for choosing which form to use is exactly the same as it was done in our previous examples. Let's practice with adjectives from each brain in the language creation lab.

Adjective Declensions 1-ý ending

	Masculine		Masculine Inanimate	
	singular	plural	singular	plural
1st	base	-+ í	=	-+é
2nd	-+ého	+ch		
3rd	-+ému	+m		
4th	-+ého	-+é	=	
5th	=	-+ í		-+é
6th	-+ém	+ých		
7th	+m	+ými		

	Feminine		Neuter	
	singular	plural	singular	plural
1st	-+á	-+é	-+é	-+á
2nd	-+é	-+ých	-+ého	-+ých
3rd	-+é	-+tým	-+ému	-+ým
4th	-+ou	-+é	-+é	-+á
5th	-+á	-+é	-+é	-+á
6th	-+é	-+ých	-+ém	-+ých
7th	-+ou	-+ými	-+m	-+ými

Adjective Declensions 2-í ending

	Masculine		Masculine Inanimate	
	singular	plural	singular	plural
1st	base	=		
2nd	+ho	+ch		
3rd	+mu	+m		
4th	+ho	=		=
5th	=	=		
6th	+m	+ch		
7th	+m	+mi		

	Feminine		Neuter	
	singular	plural	singular	plural
1st	=	=	=	=
2nd	=	+ch	+ho	+ch
3rd	=	+m	+mu	+m
4th	=	=	=	=
5th	=	=	=	=
6th	=	+ch	+m	+ch
7th	=	+mi	+m	+mi

Examples

1. She gave the black dog a bone. = Dala kost černému psovi.
2. She gave the black dogs a bone.= Dala kost černým psům.

3. The black dog is on the grass.= Černý pes je na trávě.
4. The black dogs are on the grass.= Černí psi jsou na trávě.

5. The man walked with a black dog.= Muž se procházel s černým psem.
6. The man walked with black dogs.= Muž se procházel s černými psy.

7. She took a picture of the black dog.= Viděla obrázek černého psa.
8. She took a picture of the black dogs.= Viděla obrázek černých psů.

9. She talked about the black dog.= Mluvila o černém psovi
10. She talked about the black dogs.= Mluvila o černých psech.

"This is the best pizza!"

In Section two, we learned how to form the comparative and superlative adjectives, as in bigger and the biggest.

Now let's consider some exceptions and irregulars so as to complete the picture on adjectives.

There are other groups of adjectives that form the comparative and superlative with slightly different endings and changes to the word. Since there is no way to determine to which group these adjectives belong, they need to be learned one at a time. Consequently, these adjectives will not be discussed here.

However, there are some irregulars that are so common that they are worth showing here. In English, *good* becomes *better* which becomes *best* in the superlative. Likewise, Czech also has some irregular adjectives including *good* and others, as seen below.

Some Common Irregular Adjectives

good	better	best
dobrý	lepší	nejlepší
bad	worse	worst
špatný	horší	nejhorší
big	bigger	biggest
velký	větší	největší
small	smaller	smallest
malý	menší	nejmenší
long	longer	longest
dlouhý	delší	nejdelší
much	more	most
hodně	více	nejvíce

How to create a verb brain

The Present Tense

Remember the verb brain on page 39 for the verb wait/čekat, here you will learn how all the forms were created.

Suppose you want to say something like, "We work every morning."

Step 1. If you looked up the word *work* in the mini-vocabulary list at the back of this book, you would notice that there are two words listed for the word *work*. The first is for the perfective form which will be explained later. Here we will look at the imperfective Czech word for the word *work* which is *pracovat*. (Note: Some Czech/English dictionaries are not so user friendly and may show other definitions and forms.)

Pracovat is the base form of the verb (techinically known as the infinitive) and will be used as our starting point for making all the transformations (conjugations).

There are four main classes of verbs in Czech and also some irregular verbs which don't fit into any category. Each category has varioius conjugation patterns.

Now, look at the verb charts on the next pages which show the verb classes and their endings and a sample conjugation for one of the endings each class. Since *pracovat* ends in *ovat* it belongs to the third class. Simply remove this ending *ovat* and add the endings as shown in the chart to create the Czech equivalents below. Class three has two formal forms for I and they. We will use the colloquial.

I work = pracuju
you work = pracuješ
he works = pracuje
she works = pracuje
it works = pracuje

we work = pracujeme
you work = pracujete

they work = pracují

Remember, these are the present-tense forms and are used to form ideas like "I work everyday", for habitual actions, or "I have been working for three hours", for an action that has been in progress, or "I am working", for an action in progress.

The first class verbs contain the most number of oddities. It is not always possible to predict how to form the first person singular, that is, the *I* form, but once you know the *I* form, the conjugations for the other persons follow regularly. Many books on Czech oversimplify these conjugations and generally show only one conjugation pattern for the various classes and create the impression that all verbs in those classes will behave similarly. This is not true. Take the verbs for *play* and *take* which are hrát and brát. I play is hráju but I take is beru, not bráju. In the Appendix, you will find charts which show the various ending patterns for each ending in each class and for each person, that is, the I, you, he, she, etc., forms. Most verbs will follow these patterns but there are many oddities within each class which can only be learned from a Czech speaker. :-)

In fact, various texts even list the classes differently, some show the ending patterns for the first class as the fourth class, and some show the same ending pattern in more than one class. Additionally, there are colloquial and more formal ways of expressing some of the persons, particularly the *I* and *They* form. Czech is full of irregulars, which must simply be learned as you encounter them. Ahhhhh! Get me out of here!

The vocabulary list included at the back of the book indicates the class by number and includes the first person singular form when it is irregular. If you are operating from a standard Czech/English dictionary some errors are inevitable because not enough information is given for you to determine if the verb is irregular.

The charts on the next page show one example of common ending patterns in each class. For an expanded and more complete listing and for some irregulars, see the Appendix. Four classes of verbs are shown here. Sometimes a fifth class of verbs is indicated in some Czech grammar books for the verb *to make*, or dělat in Czech, which is shown here as a first class verb. Don't ask. :-) See the Appendix page 221 for more examples.

Class 1. Verb Conjugation: verbs ending in (at or át, ít, ést, íst, éct).
Example: to make = dělat
(drop the at and add the endings shown)
I make = dělám	+ám
you make = dělát	+áš
you make = děláte plural or formal	+áte
he/she makes = dělá	+á
we make = děláme	+áme
they make = dělají	+ají

Class 2. Verb Conjugation: verbs ending in (out, ít,)
Example: to print = tisknout
(drop the out ending and add the endings shown)
I print = tisknu	+u
you print = tiskneš	+eš
you print = tisknete plural or formal	+ete
he/she prints = tiskne	+e
we print = tiskneme	+eme
they print = tisknou	+ou

Class 3. Verb Conjugation verbs ending in (ovat, ýt)

Example:
To study = studovat
(drop the ovat ending and add the endings shown)
I study = studuji (formal)	+ujii
I study = studuju (colloquial)	+uju
you study = studujete (plural or formal)	+ujete
you study = studuješ (colloquial)	+uješ
he/she studies = studuje	+uje
we study = studujeme	+ujeme
they study = studují, studujou	+uji +ujou

> **Class 4.** Verb Brain (it, et or ět)
>
> Example:
> to speak = mluvit
> (drop the *it* ending and add the endsings shown)
>
> | | |
> |---|---|
> | I speak = mluvím | +ím |
> | you speak = mluvíš | +íš |
> | you speak = mluvíte | +íte |
> | he/she speaks = mluví | +í |
> | we speak = mluvíme | +íme |
> | they speak = mluví | +í or ejí |

Now you make some conjugations in the present tense. You must first determine which class the verb belongs to and then follow the rules in the Verb Conjugation Brain.

> Language Creation Lab # 16
>
> Create a verb brain in the present tense for the verb to play (the infinitive in Czech is *hrát*).
>
> | | |
> |---|---|
> | I am playing tennis | we are playing |
> | Are you playing tennis | you are playing |
> | She is playing | |
> | He is playing | They are playing |
> | it is playing | |
>
> *Remember, in Czech, I play and I am playing, or he/she is plays/playing, etc take the same verb form.

Lab #16 Answers

I am playing tennis	hraju (hraji) tenis	we are playing hrajeme
You are playing	hraješ	(Plural) you are playing hrajete
She is playing	hraje	
He is playing	hraje	They are playing hrají
it is playing	hraje	

Comparing Czech and English Verb Tenses

Actions can be viewed in different ways. In English, for example, we have twelve ways of viewing an action.

Present	Past	Future
1. I wait	I waited	I will wait
2. I am waiting	I was waiting	I will be waiting
3. I have waited	I had waited	I will have waited
4. I have been waiting	I had been waiting	I will have been waiting

In contrast, Czech has only one verb form for the present , and only two ways of viewing the future and past. The same table in Czech, for the verb čekat (wait), looks like this.

Present	Past	Future
1. čekám	čekal jsem (imperfective)	budu čekat (imperfective)
2.	počkal jsem (perfective)	počkám (perfective)

In English, we have to choose which form of the verb to use when we make a statement. We have to know to say "He will wait for you", vs "He will be waiting for you." That is, depending on the circumstance, we have to choose between *wait* and *waiting*. We of course make this decision automatically without giving conscious thought to it, but the choice is being made imperceptibly at the subconscious level. Saying, "He will be wait for you," just doesn't sound right in English.

Likewise, in order to sound right in Czech, you will need to choose between the two verb forms in the past, if you are referring to a past action and the two in the future, if you're talking about a future action. And for now, of course, this decision will have to be a conscious one. So, how do we choose?

Our decision would be an easy one if there were a direct equivalent in meaning between the English and Czech verb aspects, but since English has four aspects and Czech only two, this will not

The imperfective and the perfective aspect

The two Czech ways of viewing an action are referred to grammatically as the *imperfective* aspect and the *perfective* aspect. (The perfective is not used in the present. It is used only to express future or past actions, while the imperfective is used in all tenses, present, past and future. Thus far, only the imperfective verbs have been used in all of the previous examples in this book.

Only the imperfective form can be used to say something like, "I am working," which is a present tense idea for an action that is in progress at the time of speaking.

The imperfective form is used for actions that are seen as open-ended or ongoing. In this way it is somewhat similar, although not always, to our *ing* form, as in "I was shopp*ing* for shoes yesterday." Viewed as an ongoing activity in the past.

In contrast, the perfective form is used for actions that convey a sense of completion or as one-time events, as in, "I will call you tonight," or "I called you yesterday," viewed as a one-time actions.

In English, we form all our verb aspects from the same base verb as it appears in the dictionary. However in Czech, you will find two entries for most Czech verbs in the dictionary.* The infinitive for the imperfective form and the infinitive for the perfective form.

If you look up some verbs in the vocabulary list at the back of this book you will find the two entries there. The first entry is the perfective infinitive and the second the imperfective infinitive. Here are a few examples:

Perfective   **Imperfective**

to call—zavolat   volat

to buy—koupit si   kupovat si

to forget—zapomenout   zapomínat

So, if you wanted to say:
"I will call you tonight." (viewed as a one time event) you would use the base perfective, zavolat and create zavolám, for "I will call", using the rules from the Verb Conjugation Brain on page 171)

"I'm a telemarketer and I will be calling people all day" (viewed as an ongoing activity in the future) Here you would use the base imperfective form, volat and create *budu* volat, for "I will be calling".

A very important point to know is that the dictionary infinitive of the perfective verb is already in the future tense.

Thus: "I will call" is zavolám (perfective future created from zavolat) and I will be calling is budu volat (imperfective future formed with the infinitive and the help of budu) If you create volám from volat, you would be saying, I call or I am calling--which is both the present simple and progressive tense in Czech.

Sometimes there is little difference in how you express an activity and you could use either verb aspect. For instance, if I say, "I will call you" or "I will be calling you," it is clear that I'm probably going to call you and you would know what I meant. The Czech language also has this flexibility in similar situations.

Before we practice choosing between the imperfective and perfective verb aspects, let's review some guidelines for their use.

The following situations only have the imperfective viewpoint.

Only the imperfective is used to express activities in the present, such as, "I am eating," etc. (with the exception of *go*, see page 183)

Some verbs have no perfective counterpart, such as,
a. to have
b. to be, být only has the imperfective future or past, I will be a teacher, Budu učitel or I was a teacher. Byl jsem učitel.
c. modal verbs such as, must, want, can, should, would, could

Now try to guess which verb aspect to use, the perfective or imperfective, in the Language Creation Lab. Circle P or I.

Language Creation Lab # 17

a) I'll see you tonight..   P/I
b) I'll see you sometime.   P/I

c) We will dance all night.   P/I
d) We will have a dance after dinner. P/I

e) Let's have a drink.   P/I
f) Every morning I drink tea.   P/I

g) They kiss each other often.   P/I
h) They have just kissed each other. P/I

Upside down answers to Lab # 17
(a-P, b-I, c-I, d-P, e-P, f-I, g-I, h-P)

Past Tense

In the People Brain on page 29 and it's duplicate on page 80, we saw the past tense forms for the verb *to be*, i.e., *I was, you were,* etc., and in the verb brain on page 39, we saw the past tense forms for čekat (to wait), which depends on which person is saying it. čekal jsem for I waited, čekala for I waited (if you are a woman), etc..Here we will learn how to create the past tense for all other verbs.

Czech has two ways of expressing past actions, with imperfective verbs and with perfective verbs. Here we will learn to create the past with imperfective verbs and on the next page with perfective verbs.

Imperfective past tense
Forming the past tense with imperfective verbs

The past tense is much easier than the present tense. Let's see how the past tense is created for čekat. The steps for creating it are as follows: First look up the verb you need in the dictionary. Look up the word wait and you will find čekat. Most all infinitives or dictionary base forms of a verb end in the letter t.

Step 1: Remove the letter t from the base form of the verb and add the letter L (known as the L-form) (or past-participle for grammar freaks) čekat becomes čekal: this is the starting point for forming the past tense, (and you will soon note that this form is also the past tense for he, she, and it waited.)

Unlike the present or future tense, the past tense changes according to whether or not the person speaking or being spoken to or about is male, female or neuter. So we need to:

- ☐ add the letter a to create the female-čekala
- ☐ add the letter o to create the neuter-čekalo
- ☐ add the letter i to create the plural-čekali
- ☐ add jsem, jsi, jsme, jste as shown below

Observe:

I waited (male) = čekal jsem
I waited (female) = čekala jsem
you waited (male) = čekal jsi
you waited (female) = čekala jsi
he waited = čekal
she waited = čekala
it waited = čekalo

we waited = čekali jsme
you waited = čekali jste
they waited = čekali

Now you try:

Language Creation Lab # 18
Past Tense
Create a past tense verb brain for the verb to to play (hrát)

I played tennis yesterday.   we played
you played   you played
he played
she played   they played
it played

(Answers on page 180)

Perfective past tense

The perfective past tense is formed from the infinitive using the same rules as for the creating the imperfective past. So if you wanted to say, "I called you yesterday," you would start with the perfective infinitive zavolat, create the I-form by dropping the t and adding an l, and then include jsem and create "zavolal jsem ti včera." (the word *ti* is one of the forms of the word *you*.)

There are some verbs which form their I-form in irregular ways and must be learned individually. Here are some of the most important ones:

	Infinitive	I-form (past-participle)
to be	být	byl
to have	mít	měl
to go	jít	šel
to eat	jíst	jedl
to want	chtít	chtěl
to give	dát	dal
to take	vzít	vzal
to read	číst	četl
to drink	pít	pil
to begin	začít	začal

These are the imperfective form of the verbs. Some verbs like, be, have and want have no perfective counterpart.

Word Order

Thus far, we have not discussed the order of words in sentences in the Czech language for two primary reasons. First, the controlled sentence patterns you learned in Section I incorporated the correct word order, so you were, without being aware of it, correctly ordering the words. Secondly, the Czech language is very forgiving when it comes to word order, because the other grammatical features of the language allow the listener to make sense of what is being said.

English in contrast has a rather rigid word order system. What is word order? The word order rules of a language say how the different parts of speech need to be arranged to make sense to other speakers of the language. Each language tends to have their own peculiarities in regards to this.

English, for example, prefers the subject to come before the verb and the object to follow the verb. For instance:

Bananas eat I, or Bananas I eat, or I bananas eat, or any arrangement other than "I eat bananas," or the subect-verb-object word order, just doesn't sound right to English speakers. In Czech, it would be possible to use each of these wordings to emphasize one or the words in the sentence, where English would do it with intonation. In Czech, the verb can float from the beginning to the end of the sentence to add emphasis to one or other word of the sentence and still sound fine to Czech speakers.

As forgiving as Czech is in regards to word order, it does have a word order hierarchy with some sentence elements.

The Second Position

If you recall, the past tense is formed with the help of jsem, jsi, etc.. As in, I was in the library—Byl jsem v knihovně. Notice that jsem is in the second position in this sentence. If for some reason I needed to emphasize the fact that I was in the library I might add já and say, "Já jsem byl v knihovně." Notice how the word order has changed slightly but that jsem has remained in the second position. The same would be true if I were talking about you and said, "Byl jsi v knihovně." The word jsi would take the second position.

So, the first word order rule states that when past tense "helping" or auxiliary words are used, words like– jsem, jsi, jsme, jste; or conditional helping words – bych, bys, by, bychom, byste, they should be placed in the second position in our sentence.

Answers Lab #18	
Včera jsem hrál tenis.	jsme hráli
jsi hrál	jste hrálí
hrál	
hrála	hráli
hrál	

The second position hierarchy rule also states that if past tense helping words are present then they will take the second position in the sentence. If they are not present then se or si will take the second position. If se or si are not present then short form dative personal pronouns will take the second position and if these are not present then accusative personal pronouns will take the second position.

For example:

"I was examining."
"Prohlížel jsem"

"I myself was examining."
"Já jsem si prohlížel."

"I was examining him."
"Prohlížel jsem si ho."

"Já jsem si ho prohlížel."
(I myself was examining him.")

Notice how the main verb *prohlížet* moved from the front to the back of the sentence.

Yes, this is very advanced and is something that you will gradually learn to use over time if you continue in the Czech language. It is included here because it is an integral part of Czech grammar and I know you want the whole story, no matter how painful.

However, don't worry about making errors here, because in context you will be understood even if you mix up this word order.

Future Tense

Czech has two primary ways of expressing the future—with the verb to be (být) and with perfective verbs, which has already been discussed . Here we will learn the rules for forming the future with the verb to be (být). (In the future tense, gender differences are not signified as they are in the past tense)

Být future

I will	budu	we will	budeme
you will	budeš	you will	budete
he will	bude		
she will	bude	they will	budou
it will	bude		

Suppose you want to say, "I will be waiting here."

The basic rule is být future + infinitive

Look in the table for I will = budu
We know that the infinitive of wait is čekat.
here = tady

So our sentence in Czech would read: "Budu čekat tady."

As in English, Czech has many ways of expressing the future. For instance, we can say, "I'm going to leave tomorrow", or "I'm leaving tomorrow", or "I leave tomorrow", or "I'll be leaving tomorrow", with little change in meaning.

Also, in English, the word *will* has several meanings and uses. For instance, it can mean willingness as in, "Will you help me?" or "I'll get that," intention and prediction.

Now you try:

Lab # 19
Create the imperfective future for the verb to play (hrát)
(Translate these phrases into Czech)

I will be playing tennis tomorrow.   We will be playing
You will be playing
He will be playing
She will be playng   They will be playing
It will be playing

Will you be playing tennis tomorrow?

(Answers on page 189)

Go

An important exception that must be mentioned is the verb *go*, which has its own way of showing its future, as shown on page 86, where the verb is conjugated. Also, there are two verbs which mean *go*. One is distinguished from the other depending on whether you are going by foot or by any other means of transport, as in planes, trains or automobiles. A mistake here is not critical and would cause some laughter if you said you were going by foot to the US from Prague, for instance. The two verbs in the infinitive are jít and jet, conjugated below.

go/jít (by foot or undefined)

I'll be going půjdu   we will be going   půjdeme
You'll be going   půjdeš   (formal/plural) půjdete
He/She/it will be going   půjde
they will be going   půjdou

go/jet (mechanical transport: car, plane, train, etc.)

I'll be going	pojedu	we will be going	pojedeme
You'll be going		pojede (formal/plural)	pojedete
He/She/it will be going		pojede	
they will be going		pojedou	

Go/Chodit

The verb Chodit is the imperfective form of jít. It's conjugations are shown on page 86.

Call me!
The Imperative

As mentioned in the verb brain on page 39, Czech uses different verb forms when using what is grammatically known as the imperative, such as when you give a command, an order or an instruction like, "wait for me", or "call me." English does not.

In English, we use the plain form of the verb *wait* whether we say, "I wait for the bus every morning" or when we say, "Wait for me." Czech creates another word to indicate the use of the imperative.

Also, imperatives can be said to either one person, as in "wait for me", or you can say the same thing to two or more people or you can include yourself and say "let's wait." Czech has three different forms to indicate each of these variations and they are formed slightly differently in each verb class and there are also exceptions within each class.

To say "Wait for me" to one person, follow these steps.

Step 1. You first need to find the "they" form (third person plural) of čekat, which is čekají.

Step 2. Drop the aji, which leavesček

Step 3. add ej, which creates čekej

To say "Wait for me" to two or more people, follow step one and two above but at step three add ejte, which creates čekejte.

To say "Let's wait," at step three add ejme which creates čekejme.

This is the pattern for all verbs in the first class. You first remove the vowel ending from the present tense "they form" and then add ej, ejte or ejme depending on the use as shown in the examples above.

These are the imperfective forms of the imperative. There are perfective variants as well in some situations.

For the third class verbs as in pracovat (to work), you drop the vowel ending from the "they form." As you know, this class has two possible *they* forms pracuji or pracujou, the former used more in written and formal Czech. Either way it leaves the same stem which is pracuj.

This form, Pracuj, is the imperative for the informal you form, no ending is added. For the formal or plural you form, add te which creates *pracujte*. For the "we" form or the let's form, add *me*, which creates pracujme.

For the first class verbs such as číst (to read), you drop the vowel ending from the they form, čtou, which leaves čt. To this, add i for the informal you form, which creates čti. For the formal or plural you form add ěte, which creates čtěte. For the let's form, add ěme, which creates čtěme.

For the fourth class verbs as in mluvit (to speak), you drop the vowel ending from the *they* form, mluví, which leaves mluv. No ending is added, thus, mluv is the informal imperative *you* form. For the plural *you* form, add te, which creates mluvte. For the let's form, add me, which creates mluvme. "Let's speak."

The most common imperatives are listed in The Language Brain on page 105.

We also form a number of imperatives with the word be, as in "Be there at seven." *Buď tam v sedm.* "Be" as the imperative is created witht the word *Buď*. If you look at the imperative chart on page 105. "Be careful" is *Buď opatrný.*

As I will be repeating throughout this book, what I have shown here is the left brain explanation of how the imperative is often formed in Czech, but how you will actually learn to use it is through hearing or reading the correct form in context and then using it through repetition, a right brain activity.

Language Creation Lab #20

Now you try creating an imperative from the verb *tell*. How would you say " Tell him." Your first step is to look up the word tell in the vocabulary list at the back of the book, and then follow the steps as outlined here.

Tell him (said to one person) =
Tell him (said to two or more people) =
Let's tell him =

Negatives:
To form the negative, the prefix *ne* is placed before the verb.

Touch this. vs. Don't touch this.
Dotýkej se toho vs. Nedotýkej se toho

(Answers on page 189)

Adverbs

In English, there are many types of adverbs and some types are used more frequently than others. Some are language engine words and are used very frequently, like: *sometimes*, *never*, *always* and *very*.

Others, such as, rapidly, loudly and kindly, are the type which are usually formed from adjectives.

Here we will learn the rules for forming adverbs from adjectives in Czech, so you can say something like "You dance divinely."

Most adverbs are formed from adjectives and most Czech adjectives end in ý or í in the first case or dictionary form.

Rule 1. if the adjective ends in dý, tý, or ný, you drop the ý ending and add the letter ě.

For example:
the adjective (beautiful) krásný becomes the adverb (beautifully) krásně.

Rule 2. If the adjective ends in lý you drop the ý ending and add the letter e. For example: the adjective rychlý (fast) becomes rychle (quickly)

Rule 3. If the adjective ends in í you usually drop the í and add ě, as in rule one above.

Some exceptions:

Some adverbs are formed by changing the ý adjective ending to the letter o. For example:

blízký becomes blízko (near)
daleký becomes daleko (far)

Adjectives that end in –ský or –cký require the adverb to end in (short) y.

Thus, the word English, as an adjective, which is anglický (long - ý), becomes anglicky (short - y) as an adverb, as in "I speak English.," Mluvím anglicky.

Comparing Adverbs

Like adjectives, adverbs can be compared. You can say for instance, that John drives carefully, but that Tom drives more carefully than John. And that Joe drives the most carefully of them all.

Czech allows these same sorts of comparisons and here's how it's done.

1. Starting with a regular adverb like krásně (beautifully), you first remove the last letter, which creates krásn.
2. To this you add ěji which creates krásněji, the comparative, or in English, more beautifully.
3. To create the superlative, you simply add the prefix nej which creates nejkrásněji, the most beautifully.
With adverbs that end in o, eko, or oko you first:

a. drop the ending - so with an adverb like daleko (far) you create –dal
b. lengthen the vowel if it isn't already and create- dál
c. or, if after you remove the ending you end with a root that ends in a hard consonant, you change it to its soft counterpart - for example: with an adverb like blízko (near) you create blíz, then change the z to a ž, which creates blíž.

d. then add an e which creates dále and blíže, for farther and nearer respectively.
e. to create the superlative you simply add the prefix nej, which creates nejblíže and nejdále for the furthest and nearest.

There are of course, some oddballs and irregulars which include:

well	dobře	lépe	nejlépe
badly	špatně	hůře	nejhůře
early/soon	brzo	dříve	nejdříve
small/little	málo	méně	nejméně
long	dlouho	déle	nejdéle
much	mnoho	více	nejvíce
easily	snadno	snáze	nejsnáze

Lab #19
Answers

I will be playing tennis tomorrow.	Zítra budu hrát tenis.
Will you be playing tennis tomorrow?	Budeš hrát zítra tenis?
He will be playing	Bude hrát.
She will be playng	Bude hrát.
It will be playing	Bude hrát.
We will be playing	Budeme hrát.
You will be playing	Budete hrát.
They will be playing	Budou hrát.

Lab #20
Answers

Tell him (said to one person) = řekni mu. Don't tell him= neříkej mu.
Tell him (said to two or more people) = řekněte mu.
Let's tell him = řekněme mu.

What's the date today? Part 2
Kolikátého je dnes?

In English, you could respond to the above question in one of two ways:

You could say : "It's October 22, or "It's the 22nd of October."

In the bad Czech section, On page 68, we learned how to say the first version above. Je říjen dvacátý druhý.

Here we will learn the second way.

On page 133, we discussed some of the reasons for making case changes. There it mentions that phrases in English with the word *of* often call for the use of the genitive case in Czech. So our steps for translating the 22nd of October are as follows:

1. Create the genitive for October/ říjen. For your convenience we have included the genitive forms for all of the months because there were too many exceptions to form them consistently from any rules. That's language for you. :-) Worth knowing, however, is that all the months, except for September (září) are masculine hard inanimate nouns and they belong to the special group whose genitive ends in –a rather than –u. (with some exceptions)

2. Numbers are considered adjectives and, as always, adjectives must agree with the noun's gender, number and case. We know the gender, MHI, the case is genitive, the number is singular, so we must transform the 22nd (dvacátý druhý) to match each of these conditions. Look in the Adjective brain on page 165 for adjectives that end in ý. Here we see that we must add the end *ého*. So, the 22nd of October becomes, *dvacátého druhého října*.

Months

	Nominative	Genitive
January	leden	ledna
February	únor	února
March	březen	března
April	duben	dubna
May	květen	května
June	červen	června
July	červenec	července
August	srpen	srpna
September	září	září
October	říjen	října
November	listopad	listopadu
December	prosinec	prosince

SPEAK CZECH BADLY! BUT SPEAK IT TODAY!

Using Modal Verbs in Czech

"You **should** eat more spinach."
"We **could** play tennis next week."
"I **should** have called her."
"We **could** have gone to Paris."

The statements above express the speaker's suggestion, advice, preference or possibilities. The next few pages will show how these types of thoughts are expressed in Czech.

Should

Should is used primarily by the speaker to suggest the advisability of something as in "You should stop smoking." It is also used to state an expectation or guess, as in "We should be there by seven," or "He should win the race."

In Czech, these ideas are expressed with the word combinations shown below.

Should Brain #1

(present advisability or expectation)

I should = Měl bych   We should = Měli bychom or *bysme
You should = Měl bys   You should = Měli byste
he should = Měl by
she should = Měla by   They should = Měli by
it should = Mělo by

I shouldn't (to form the negative simply add the letters 'ne' before the first word, thus: I shouldn't = **ne**měl bych
To make a question, simply use the same word order with a rising intonation: Should I …?- Měl bych..?

Should + plus the infinitive form of the verb is used to express these ideas, as in English.
*colloquial use in Prague

Language Creation Lab # 21

These are the infinitives and vocabulary to help you create these sentences. stop smoking = přestat kouřit, call his mother = zavolat své matce, be here at seven = být tady v sedm.

1. You should stop smoking.
2. He should call his mother.
3. She should be here at seven.

(Answers on page 200)

Should have Brain #2 (past advisability, expectation)

I should have = Měl jsem   We should have = Měli jsme
You should have = Měl(a) jsi   You should have = Měli jste, (mixed gender group) měly jste (all females) měla jste (neuter)
he should have = Měl
she should have = Měla   They should have = Měli, Měly, Měla
it should have = Mělo
negative = I shouldn't have = neměl jsem
yes/no question = Should I have...? same order- měl jsem..?

Should have + Infinitive

We can make the same statements using *should* about past actions. As in, "He should have called his mother." In English, we create the past idea by adding the word *have* after the word *should*. The construction in Czech for stating the past use of *should* is shown above.

In English we use the past participle form of the verb that follows *should have*, as in, should have *called*, should have *eaten*, etc. Czech uses the infinitive form of the verb after *should have*. For example: "He shouldn't have said that." = "Neměl to říkat."

(říkat is the infinitive of say.)

For the most part, we can use the same word order as we do in English. Although in the above Czech version, *that-to* comes before *say*, however, you would be understood if you placed it after *say*. However, see page 179 for important notes on the use of jsem in the word order of Czech sentences.

Language Creation Lab 22

1. He should have called his mother.
2. She should have been here at seven.
(Answers on page 200)

Could

In English, we use the word could when making polite requests as in "Could you shut the door please?", when talking about a past ability, "I could run faster when I was a child.", when considering possibilities, as in, "We could eat pizza tonight.", and the same idea in the past, as in, "We could have eaten pizza last night." In Section two, we learned how to make polite requests with *could* using some of the constructions in the Could Brain 1 below. Here, let's practice creating sentences that suggest possibilities or alternatives.

Could Brain#1—Possibilities & polite requests
"We could go to the cinema tonight."(possibility)
"Could you help me?"(request)

I could = mohl bych   we could = mohli bychom
you could = mohl bys   you could = mohli byste
he could = mohl by
she could = mohla by   they could = mohli by
it could = mohlo by

I couldn't = nemohl bych
Could I ? = Mohl bych..?   Could + Infinitive
(See Appendix for male/female differences in the plural)

Language Creation Lab 23

1. We could go to the cinema tonight.
2. You could take the train.
(Answers on page 200)

Could Brain #2 - Past ability and past possibilities

"I could run faster as a child."(past ability)
"We could have gone to the cinema last night."
(past possibility)

I could = mohl jsem   we could = mohli jsme
you could = mohl(a) jsi   you could = mohli jste
he could = mohl
she could = mohla   they could = mohli
it could = mohlo

I couldn't = nemohl jsem
I couldn't have = nemohl jsem
Asking about past ability or possibility: mohl jsem..?
                         Could have + Infinitive

Examples

I could have eaten more.   Mohl jsem sníst více.

We could have gone to the cinema.   Mohli jsme jít do kina.

We could have taken the train.   Mohli jsme jet vlakem.

Would

In English, *Would* has several uses. In polite requests and offers, such as, "Would you help me?," "Would you like some water?" In imaginary or conditional sentences, such as, "I would do it like this", "I would rather…", "I wish it would…","If I were rich, I would by a castle. And it is the past of will in English, as in, "He said he would be here at 7." , but not in Czech, where they still use will and say "He said, he *will* be here at 7." The instructions for making offers, invitations and requests with *would* was introduced on page 54, Here we will explore other uses of this versatile word. Do remember that the equal sign is not a literal word equivalent but a meaning and usage equivalent.

Would Brain

Would/would have

I would = já bych   we would = my bychom
you would = ty bys   you would = vy byste
he would = on by
she would = ona by   they would = oni by
it would = to/ono by (*ono* is used more for living things)

I would do it different\ly. (imaginary present or future)
I would have done it differently. (imaginary past)

(Although Czech does have a grammar for creating the past intention structure, Czech speakers typically just use the imaginary future idea for both imaginary future and past ideas and let the context of the conversation clarify the meaning, or add a paste tense time word, like yesterday or last week, etc. Consequently, we will show only one construction here that you can use for either idea.)

How it is formed: Past tense L form + bych
Examples

I would do it differently. = udělal bych to jinak.
I would have done it differently. = udělal bych to jinak. (same grammar, context tells the speaker that it was in the past)

"If I were rich, I would buy a castle."
Using conditionals

We often express thoughts that consist of a statement and a condition for that statement, such as, "If I were rich, I would buy a castle." These types of statements consist of two parts. The *if* part, which is the condition, and the proclamation part, or what you would do if the condition were met. The two parts are often separated by a comma. In English we often use *would* or *could* in the other clause and you can do the same in Czech.

The formula for creating this type of conditional statement in Czech is shown below. Unlike English, Czech uses the L-form (past participle) in both parts, ie., English uses the infinitive *buy* and Czech uses the past participle *bought*. Also notice that bych is in the second position in the second part.

If I	kdybych	If we	kdybychom
If you	kdybys	If you	kdybyste
If he/she/it	kdyby	If they	kdyby

"If I were rich, I would buy a castle."
Kdybych byl bohatý, koupil bych si hrad.

How it is formed: Kdybych + L form, + L form verb + bych

Examples

If I had a a car, I would save time. Kdybych měl auto, ušetřil bych čas.

If he had a job, he would have money. Kdyby měl práci, měl by peníze.

If you exercised more, you would lose weight. Kdybys více cvičil, zhubnul bys.

"I wish ..."

Language Creation Lab

I wish I = kéž bych   I wish we = kéž bychom
I wish you = kéž bys   I wish you = kéž byste
I wish he/she/it = kéž by   I wish they = kéž by

I wish it wasn't so cold.   Kéž by nebyla taková zima.

(I wish = kéž) + correct form of by + past tense

* (The verb přát si, and the noun přání also mean *wish* in Czech)

"If I see him, I will tell him."

This future conditional idea consists of the "if part" and the other part.

The Czech language has two ways of expressing the word *if*. The first is when *If* is combined with a subject pronoun, as in If I = kdybych, If you = kdybys, etc., which we just looked at on the previous page. The other way to say *if* is with the word *Jestli*. Jestli is used for future conditional ideas.

Jestli + the future perfective verb form is used in both the *if* and second clause of the sentence.

Example

If I see him, I will tell him. = Jestli ho uvidím, řeknu mu to.

(uvidím and řeknu are both in the future perfective verb form)

Aby clauses

Czech has an additional language feature that is used primarily to show the reason or purpose for doing something. It is quite often used in statements where English speakers might say, so or so that, to or in order to, or for. For example, an English speaker might say:

"I put on a sweater so that I wouldn't be cold."

so that I	abych	so that we	abychom
so that you	abys	so that you	abyste
so that he	aby	so that they	aby
so that she	aby	so that they	aby
so that it	aby	so that they	aby

Another use for Aby is when, in English we might say, "I want you to leave, or I would like you to leave." You can not directly translate "I want you to..."to Czech, however, we could express the same thought using the phrase "for you", as in, " I would like *for you* to leave." Here Czech uses Aby.

"He would like me to leave."
"He would like for me to leave."

for me to	abych	for us to	abychom
for you to	abys	for you to	abyste
for him to	aby	for them to	aby
for her to	aby	for them to	aby
for it to	aby	for them to	aby

These aby clauses are used in a variety of situations, for wishes, requests and advice (using want, would like, need, tell and ask) This is one of those language features that require more experience with the language to know when to use. Remember though, that there is always more than one way to communicate a thought in any language.

More Examples:
I want you to stop smoking.   Chci, abys přestal kouřit.
(I would like for you to stop smoking.)

It's too early to leave.   Je příliš brzy odejít.
(It's too early for us to leave) Je moc brzy na to, abychom odešli.

Lab Answers

Lab #21
You should stop smoking.= měl bys přestat kouřit.
He should call his mother.= měl by zavolat své matce.
She should be here at seven.= měla by tady být v sedm.

Lab #22
He should have called his mother.=Měl zavolat své matce.
She should have been here at seven.= Měla tady být v sedm.

Lab #23
We could go to the cinema tonight.= Dnes večer bychom mohli jít do kina.
You could take the train.= Mohl bys jet vlakem.

Telling the time Part 2
Half past/Quarter past and Quarter to the Hour

On page 64, we learned how to give the time in minutes on the hour and minutes *to* and *past* the hour. Here we will learn how to say half past, a quarter past and a quarter *to* the hour. For this we need the genitive case, and ordinal numbers.

Czech and English view quarters and halves of hours in opposite ways. In English, we view 5:30 for instance, as half past five. But Czech speakers view it as "half towards six." The semi-literal translation is "half of the sixth hour." Being a part of something requires ordinal numbers and the genitive case.

Half Past

Example:
"It is half past three." (Literally in Czech, "It is half towards the fourth hour.")

je = it is,   half = půl,   four in the genitive = čtvrté

So, "It is half past three." = je půl čtvrté

Quarter past : In the same way, a quarter after or past is viewed in Czech as a quarter towards the next hour. However, Czech speakers now say, "it is a quarter on the next hour", not a quarter of. As we learned in the section which discuses more reasons for making case changes, the use of prepositions usually affects the case of the noun which follows. In this situation, Czech speakers include the preposition on—na, to say *on* the next hour, which requires the number which follows to be put into the accusative form and the use of cardinal, not ordinal numbers.

For example: Let's say it is a quarter past five.

je = it is   a quarter on= čtvrt na six (accusative form) = šest

a quarter past five = *je čtvrt na šest.*

With the exception of numbers one and two, jeden and dva, numbers in the accusative case are the same as the nominative case. Thus no changes are made to the number six or šest in Czech.

A Quarter to: If you haven't guessed, a quarter to the hour is viewed in Czech as a three quarters towards the next hour. It is also worded as three quarters on the next hour. So, when we say it is a quarter to six Czech speakers would say it is three quarters on six. Finally, we need the plural for quarter to say three quarters, which is čtvrtě.

Let's try it:

It is a quarter to six.

je = it is
three quarters on= tři čtvrtě na
six (accusative form) = šest

je tři čtvrtě na šest

Telling the time part 2
More Examples

1. It's a quarter to two. Je tři čtvrtě na dvě.
2. It's 3:30 pm. Je půl čtvrté.
3. It's a quarter past four. Je čtvrt na pět.

"They have a daughter, who lives in Brazil."
(relative clauses)

In English we can say, "The man who lives next door is an alien." We can make the same statement and use the word *that* instead of *who* without changing the meaning. Observe: "The man that lives next door is an alien." We use *that* and *who* in these types of sentences when referring to people and *which* or *that*, when we refer to things as in, "I like the film which/ that starred Mel Gibson."

The Czech language simply uses the word který (which) in both of these types of sentences. So Czech speakers would say,

"The man který lives next door is an alien."
"I like the film který starred Mel Gibson."

For bad Czech, you can use který in all these situations and be understood. Gold Medal Czech however, requires the word který to change form. As an adjective, který will change form according to the gender of the noun that follows it. All the changes are shown in the table on the next page.

Which sweater do you like?   Který svetr se ti líbí?
Which book do you like?   Která kniha se ti líbí?
Which car do you like?   Které auto se ti líbí?

They have a daughter who lives in Brazil.=
Mají dceru, která žije v Brazílii.

  * Note the comma before the word *which*. In Czech, a comma is always used to separate relative clauses in statements.

SPEAK CZECH BADLY! BUT SPEAK IT TODAY!

Who and What change form too!

In Section I, in the Question word chart on page 48, you learned that the Czech words for *who* and *what* are *kdo* and *co*, respectively. But as these question words refer to people and things, they can play different grammatical roles, and in Czech, they change form accordingly.

The word *Who* can translate to: **Kdo, koho, komu, koho, o kom, and s kým.**

The word *What* can translate to: **co, čeho, čemu, o čem and s čím**

See them transform in the examples below.

Nominative
1st Who is that?   **Kdo** je to?
1st What is that?   **Co** je to?

Genitive
2nd Who can't you live without?   Bez **koho** nemůžeš žít?
2nd What can't you live without?   Bez **čeho** nemůžeš žít?

Dative
3rd Who will you tell?   **Komu** to řekneš?
3rd What are you laughing at?   **Čemu** se směješ?

Accusative
4th Who do you know?   **Koho** znáš?
4th What are you doing?   **Co** děláš?

Locative
6th Who are you talking about?   **O kom** mluvíš?
6th What are you talking about?   **O čem** mluvíš?

Instrumental
7th Who did you go with? **S kým** jsi šel? (With whom did you go?)
7th What are you writing with? **Čím** píšeš? (With what are you writing?)

*Knowing what changes form, and when to make case changes is for "Gold Medal" students of the Czech language. For "Bad Czech" purposes you can simply use Kdo and Co in each of the examples above and be understood.

The word "Which" changes form according to case and gender.

Singlular	masc	fem	neuter
1st. case	který	která	které
2nd. case	kterého	které	kterého
3rd. case	Kterému	které	kterému
4th. case	(Inanimate) (Animate) Který/ kterého	kterou	které
5th. case	-	-	-
6th. case	O kterém	o které	o kterém
7th. case	S kterým	s kterou	s kterým
Plural	(Inanimate) (Animate)		
1st. case	Které/ kteří	které	která
2nd. case	Kterých	kterých	kterých
3rd. case	Kterým	kterým	kterým
4th. case	Které	které	která
5th. case	-	-	-
6th. case	O kterých	o kterých	o kterých
7th. case	S kterými	s kterými	s kterými

"What kind of...?" changes form according to case and gender.

"What kind of car do you like? or Which kind of car do you like?

The question word *jaký* is also an adjective and changes form according to the gender, number and case of the noun it refers to.

What kind of man?	Jaký muž?
What kind of woman?	Jaká žena?
What kind of apple?	Jaké jablko?

Singlular	masculine	feminine	neuter
1st. case	jaký	jaká	jaké
2nd. case	jakého	jaké	jakého
3rd. case	jakému	jaké	jakému
4th. case	(Inanimate) (Animate)		
	jaký/ jakého	jakou	jaké
5th. case	-	-	-
6th. case	O jakém	o jaké	o jakém
7th. case	S jakým	s jakou	s jakým
Plural	(Inanimate) (Animate)		
1st. case	Jaký-jaké	jaké	jaká
2nd. case	Jakých	jakých	jakých
3rd. case	jakým	jakým	jakým
4th. case	jaké	jaké	jaká
5th. case	-	-	-
6th. case	o jakých	o jakých	o jakých
7th. case	s jakými	s jakými	s jakými

How Numbers Change Form

The numbers in the number chart on page 60, are all in the nominative case, but numbers too change form and they have their own peculiar rules for doing so. They change form in six of the seven cases (the vocative case is not applicable) and numbers one and two also change form according to the broad gender categories, that is, only in three categories: masculine, feminine and neuter. (There is a great deal of repetition in the forms in each of the cases as you will see.) See the rules and brains below.

Rule 1. The number one changes form in all the cases according to gender and case.

Numeral 1 Brain

	masculine/MI	feminine	neuter
nominative	jeden	jedna	jedno
genitive	jednoho	jedné	jednoho
dative	jednomu	jedné	jednomu
accusative	jednoho/jeden	jednu	jedno
locative	jednom	jedné	jednom
instrumental	jedním	jednou	jedním

Examples: How the number one changes form in each case.

1st case
Masculine : One table is red.   *Jeden* stůl je červený.
Feminine: One book is red.   *Jedna* kniha je červená.
Neuter: One apple is red.   *Jedno* jablko je červené.

Examples: How the number one changes form in each case and gender.

2nd case
M: He left without one table. Odešel bez toho jednoho stolu.
F: He left without one book. Odešel bez té jedné knihy.
N: He left without one apple. Odešel bez toho jednoho jablka.

3rd case
M: He gave the money to one man.
Dal peníze jednomu pánovi.
F: He gave the money to one women.
Dal peníze jedné ženě.
N: He gave the money to one baby.
Dal peníze jednomu dítěti.

4th case
M: He has one table.
Má jeden stůl.
F: He has one book.
Má jednu knihu.
N: He has one apple.
Má jedno jablko.

6th case
M: He thought about one table.
Přemýšlel o jednom stole.
F: He thought about one book.
Přemýšlel o jedné knize.
N: He thought about one apple.
Přemýšlel o jednom jablku.

7th case
M: He left with one table.
Odešel s jedním stolem.
F: He left with one book.
Odešel s jednou knihou.
N: He left with one apple.
Odešel s jedním jablkem.

Rule 2. The number two changes form in only the nominative and accusative case according to gender and in all other cases according only to case.

Numeral 2 Brain

	Masc	Fem	Neuter
nominative	dva	dvě	dvě
genitive	dvou		
dative	dvěma		
accusative	dva	dvě	dvě
locative	dvou		
instrumental	dvěma	dvěmi	

Examples with the number two

1st case
Masculine: Two tables are red.   Dva stoly jsou červené.
Feminine: Two books are red.   Dvě knihy jsou červené.
Neuter: Two apples are red.   Dvě jablka jsou červená.

2nd case
M: The legs of two tables are red. Nohy dvou stolů jsou červené.
F: The covers of two books are red. Obaly dvou knih jsou červené.
N: The skins of two apples are red. Slupky dvou jablek jsou červené.

3rd case
M: He gave the money to two man. Dal peníze dvěma mužům.
F: He gave the money to two women. Dal peníze dvěma ženám.
N: He gave the money to two babies. Dal peníze dvěma dětem.

4th case
M: He has two tables.   Má dva stoly.
F: He has two books.   Má dvě knihy.
N: He has two apples.   Má dvě jablka.

6th case
M: He thought about two tables.   Přemýšlel o dvou stolech.
F: He thought about two books.   Přemýšlel o dvou knihách.
N: He thought about two apples.   Přemýšlel o dvou jablkách.

7th case
M: He left with two tables.   Odešel se dvěma stoly.
F: He left with two books.   Odešel se dvěmi knihami.
N: He left with two apples.   Odešel se dvěma jablky.

Rule 3. The numbers 3 and above disregard gender and change form according only to case.

Numerals 3 and 4 Brain

nominative	tři	čtyři
genitive	tři	čtyř
dative	třem	čtyřem
accusative	tři	čtyři
locative	třech	čtyřech
instrumental	třemi	čtyřmi

Numbers 5 and above use the same ending pattern. These numbers simply add the letter i in all but the first and fourth case. Number six has been included as an example.

Numerals 5-99

nominative	pět	šest
genitive	pěti	šesti
dative	pěti	šesti
accusative	pět	šest
locative	pěti	šesti
instrumental	pěti	šesti

As gender is disregarded from numbers three and above, you can simply use the same examples as before and substitute any number you need and simply change its form in each of the cases.

For example:
1st case
Three tables are red. Tři stoly jsou červené.
Four men are red. Čtyři muži jsou červení.
Four apples are red. Čtyři jablka jsou červená.
Five apples are red. Pět jablek je červených. (plural genetive for both apples and red and *are* changes to *is*)

2nd case
The legs of three tables are red. Nohy tří stolů jsou červené.
The covers of four books are red. Obaly čtyř knih jsou červené.
The skins of five apples are red. Slupky pěti jablek jsou červené.

3rd case
He gave the money to three men. Dal peníze třem mužům.
He gave the money to four women. Dal peníze čtyřem ženám.
He gave the money to five babies. Dal peníze pěti dětem.

4th case
He has three tables. Má tři stoly.
He has four books. Má čtyři knihy.
He has five apples. Má pět jablek.

6th case
He thought about three tables. Myslel na tři stoly.
He thought about four books. Myslel na čtyři knihy.
He thought about five apples. Myslel na pět jablek.

7th case
He left with three tables. Odešel se třemi stoly.
He left with four books. Odešel se čtyřmi knihami.
He left with five apples. Odešel s pěti knihami.

More Numbers

"One pair of pants"

Some words have plural endings even when they are singular in number, like one pair of pants, or eye glasses for instance.

Czech numbers change to mark these types of singular items that typically consist of two parts and are referred to in the plural. Words like these in Czech include: pants, eye glasses, shoes,

one pair of pants	jedny kalhoty
two pairs of pants	dvoje
three pairs of pants	troje
four pairs of pants	čtvery
five pairs of pants	patery
six pairs of pants	šestery
seven pairs of pants	sedmery
eight pairs of pants	osmery
nine pairs of pants	devatery
ten pairs of pants	desatery
eleven pairs of pants	jedenáctery
twelve pairs of pants	dvanáctery

Even More Numbers
"Tram 22"

In spoken colloquial Czech, you will often hear numbers change yet again when referring to numbered items as in "Tram 22", or hotel rooms for instance. These numbers look like this:

room 1 pokoj jednička
room 2 pokoj dvojka
room 3 pokoj trojka
room 4 pokoj čtyřka
room 5 pokoj pětka

room 6 pokoj šestka
room 7 pokoj sedmička
room 8 pokoj osmička
room 9 pokoj devítka
room 10 pokoj desitka

Money - Penize

cash - hotovost   coins - mince   change - drobný

Much in the same way the slang word *buck* is used for a dollar, Czechs sometimes say *stovka* to refer to one hundred crowns notes.

100 crowns = stovka (when referrring to a hundred crown note)
Give me a 100 crown note = Dej mi stovku
(the word *stovka* changes to the third case form, *stovku* after the verb *give*)

(check the currency exchange rate, this is just a grammar exercise)

one hundred - jedna stovka
two one hundred bills- dvě stovky
three one hundred bills - tři stovky
four one hundred bills - čtyři stovky
five one hundred bills - pět stovek (from five on up you say *stovek*)

Czech has a two hundred, five hundred, one thousand, two thousand, and five thousand crown bills.(see Appendix for more on money)

Se and Si Revisted (part 2)

On page 80, you were introduced to the ever-present particle *se*. Here we will look more closely at *se* and its counterpart *si*. Very broadly, *se* and *si* are used in the following ways:

1. si and se appear with some verbs as part of the verb. For example: the verb "to decide" is *rozhodnout se*. You will encounter several of these types of verbs in the vocabulary list at the end of the book and in the list of verbs on starting on page 93.

2. se creates the reflexive idea, as in, "How are you?" or in Czech "How are you having yourself" as mentioned earlier. Or in a statement like "He sees himself in the mirror."
Also, se changes form in some of the cases, see below: (se changes to si in the dative or 3rd case)

2nd They can't live without each other.	Nemůžou bez **sebe** žít.
3rd She bought herself an orange.	Koupila **si** pomeranč.
4th I am well.	Mám **se** dobře.
6th He talks only about himself.	Mluví jenom o **sobě**.
7th Bring it with you. (yourself)	Přines to s **sebou**.

3. *se* can be used to create the passive (see next page)

4. (And don't forget that *se*, used before words starting with s or *s* between words, can also mean *with*)

nominative	not used in the nominative or locative
genitive	sebe
dative	si-sobě
accusative	se/sebe
locative	sobě
instrumental	sebou

As mentioned earlier, there is usually more than one way to express any thought. So, there is another word in Czech which is used for instances where you might say, "They are visiting each other = Navštívili se *navzájem. T*he word *navzájem* is used here to express the "each other" idea.

Passive Speech

In the sentences we have looked at so far, the object of the sentence received the action of the verb. It is possible, however, to construct sentences where the subject receives the action of the verb. For instance, we can say, "John called the police," or "The police were called." In the first sentence we know that John did the calling and that the police were the receivers of that call. In the second sentence, the police were also called but we don't know who called them. Sentences in which the subject receives the action rather than being the cause of the action are called passive. In English, if you want to keep the sentence in the passive form, but still say who performed the action we can add "by" and say "The police were called by John."

In English, we form the passive with the help of the verb "to be" and the past participle. For example, "were called", from the example in the paragraph above, "called" is the regular past participle.

The primary way the passive is expressed in Czech is also with the verb to be (být) plus the passive participle, or the "n/t-participle" because of the two types of endings used to form it. See the charts next page for the verbs "beat, and make/do". The verb changes endings depending on the gender of the object receiving the action of the verb.

Singular

	Masculine	Feminine	Neuter
to beat	zbit	zbita	zbito
to make	dělán	dělána	děláno

The man was beaten. Muž byl zbit.
The woman was beaten. Žena byla zbita.

The verb *to beat* exists in both the imperfective and perfective forms, bit and zbit respectively. So, to say "He is being beaten," which is a present tense idea, you would say, "Je bit."

Plural

	Masculine	Feminine	Neuter
to beat	biti	bity	bita
to make	děláni	dělány	dělána

The passive can be used in every tense. For example, we can say:

"It was built."   "Bylo postaveno."
"It is being built." "Je staveno."
"It will be built."   "Bude postaveno."

In Czech, you simply use be-být in each tense, was-bylo, is-je, and will be-bude plus the passive participle form of the verb. The passive imperfective form of *built* in Czech is *staveno* and the perfective is postaveno.

Czech can also create the passive idea with the relflexive particle *se*.

"It isn't done that way." = "Ono se neudělalo."
"How is it written. = "Jak se to píše."

There is much more which could be said about the Czech passive but since it is used primarily in written Czech, we will end our discussion here. The active form can almost always be used and is far easier to construct.

Terms of Endearment
Diminutives

As the Czech language contains mechanisms for converting almost any word into a diminutive, it quite possibly has more terms of endearment than any other language. You may be baffled by hearing a word that you think you know, only to find out later that it was in its diminutive form.

Diminutives are of two types, those which are nicknames such as William becoming Billy and those which refer to smaller versions of an item, such as "booklet", which refers to a small book. In Czech, these word alterations are typically accomplished by adding endings such as , -ek,- ík,-eček, -íček, or -ínek to masculine nouns and various modifications to female names with an eventual -a ending.
Examples:

The name Jana can become Janička.

The name Adéla becomes Adélka.

The name Petr becomes Petřík, and so on.

This affectionate tinkering with words and names is more of an art than science and it is being brought to your awareness so that instead of being baffled by what you think are new words, you should realize that endearing diminutives are being dished out in ample servings. Enjoy.

*As in English, these diminutive forms are often used with children and sometimes adults do not like being called by these forms. So, it is best to get permission to use these cute forms.

Appendix

Demonstrative Adjectives

To astonish or frighten you, the charts seen here are the myriad forms of this/that/these and those in the Czech language. The forms below are used in writing and formal spoken Czech. There are repetitions and some overlap with the colloquial uses in the chart on the facing page.

case			MA	MI	F	N
1st	singular	this here/that there	tento/tamten	tento/tamten	tato/tamta	toto/tamto
	plural	these here/those there	tito/tamti	tyto/tamty	tyto/tamty	tyto/tamta
2nd	singular	this here/that there	tohoto/tamtoho		této/tamté	tohoto/tamtoho
	plural	these here/those there	těchto/tamtěch		těchto/tamtěch	těchto/tamtěch
3rd	singular	this here/that there	tomuto/tamtomu		této/tamté	tomuto/tamtomu
	plural	these here/those there	těmto/tamtěm		těmto/tamtěm	těmto/tamtěm
4th	singular	this here/that there	tohoto/tamtoho	tento/tamten	tuto/tamtu	toto/tamto
	plural	these here/those there	tyto/tamty	tyto/tamty	tuto/tamty	tato/tamta
6th	singular	this here/that there	tamto/tamtom		této/tamté	tomto/tamto
	plural	these here/those there	těchto/tamtěch		těchto/tamtěch	těchto/tamtěch
7th	singular	this here/that there	tímto/tamtím		touto/tamtou	tímto/tamtím
	plural	these here/those there	těmito/tamtěmi		těmito/tamtěmi	těmito/tamtěmi

Appendix
Colloquial-Informal usage

case			MA	MI	F	N
1st	singular	this here/that there	tenhle/tamhleten	tyhle/tamhlety	tahle/tamhleta	tohle/tamhleto
	plural	these here/those there	tihle/tamhleti		tyhle-tamhlety	tahle-tamhleta
2nd	singular	this here/that there	tohohle/tamhletoho		téhle/tamhleté	tomhle/tamhletom
	plural	these here/those there	těchhle/tamhletěch		těchhle/tamhletěch	těchhle/tamhletěch
3rd	singular	this here/that there	tomuhle/tamhletomu		téhle/tamhleté	tomuhle/tamhletomu
	plural	these here/those there	těmhle/tamhletěm		těmhle/tamhletěm	těmhle/tamhletěm
4th	singular	this here/that there	tohohle/tamhletoho	tenhle/tamhleten	tuhle/tamhletu	tohle/tamhletoho
	plural	these here/those there	tyhle/tamhlety		tyhle/tamhlety	tahle-tamhleta
6th	singular	this here/that there	tomhle/tamhletom		téhle/tamhleté	tomhle/tamhletom
	plural	these here/those there	těchhle/tamhletěch		těchhle/tamhletěch	těchhle/tamhletěch
7th	singular	this here/that there	timhle/tamhletim		touhle/tamhletou	timhle/tamhletim
	plural	these here/those there	těmihle/tamhletěmi		těmihle/tamhletěmi	těmihle/tamhletěmi

Czech Prefixes and Suffixes

Like English, Czech has many prefixes and suffixes which alter the meaning or form of the word to which they are attached. It would be nice but misleading to say that certain prefixes or suffixes change the meaning of a word in predictable ways but this just simply isn't the case as there are too many exceptions. I believe it is best to learn each word separately to avoid mistakes.

That said, here is a short list of common Czech prefixes and suffixes.

Common Czech prefixes: do-, o-, od-, po-, pod-, pře-, před-, roz-, u-, v-, vy-, z-, za.

Common Czech suffixes:

Some feminine words are formed from the masculine counterpart by adding the suffix "-ka or if the word ends in a consonant. If the masculine form ends with –k, the feminine ending is formed by adding –čka or -ice Student becomes studentka, ředitel (director masc.) becomes ředitelka (director, f).

If the masculine form ends in a vowel, -í, the feminine form stays the same: Vrchní (head waiter) can be male or female.

Customarily, feminine forms of surnames are formed by the suffix –ová. Novák -- Nováková,
Often the Czech media uses this grammar to "feminize" even English surnames: Harper becomes Harperová, Marilyn -Monroeová

And of course, we already encountered how verb endings show personal pronoun changes. See next page for more on this.

APPENDIX

Verb Classes and their conjugations

These are the major conjugations for verbs with these endings, as mentioned previously, there are exceptions and some Czech grammar books may classify them differently.

> ## Class 1. Verb Conjugation Brain
> verbs ending in (at, át, ít, ést, íst, éct)

Class 1. Infintive	nést	číst	péct	třít	brát	mazat
Present tense	nesu neseš nese nesem(e) nesete nesou	čtu čteš čte čtem(e) čtete čtou	peču pečeš peče pečem(e) pečete pečou	třu třeš tře třem(e) třete třou	beru bereš bere berem(e) berete berou	mažu mažeš maže mažem(e) mažete mažou
Past participle	nesl	četl	pekl	třel	bral	mazal

221

Class 2. Verb Conjugation Brain verbs ending in (out, ít,)

Class 2. Infinitive	tisknout	minout	začít
Present tense	tisknu tiskneš tiskne tisknem(e) tisknete tisknou	minu mineš mine minem(e) minete minou	začnu začneš začne začnem(e) začnete začnou
Past participle	tiskl	minul	začal

Class 3. Verb Conjugation Brain verbs ending in (ovat, ýt)

Class 3. Infinitive	krýt	kupovat
Present tense	kryji, kryju kryješ kryje kryjem(e) kryjete kryjí, kryjou	kupuji, kupuju kupuješ kupuje kupujem(e) kupujete kupují, kupujou
Past participle	kryl	kupoval

Class 4. Verb Brain (it, et or ět)

Class 4. Infinitive	prosit	čistit	trpět	sázet
Present tense	prosím prosíš prosí prosíme prosíte prosí	čistím čistíš čistí čistíme čistíte čistí	trpím trpíš trpí trpíme trpíte trpí	sázím sázíš sází sázíme sázíte sázejí, sází
Past participle	prosil	čistil	trpěl	sázel

Most of the Verbs in this book expanded

The list here includes the "I" and "you" form and the past participle. The first verb listed in bold is the **future perfective** form and the second the **imperfective**. Some verbs have only one form in common usage, so only one is shown. Remember that you can simply use "Budu" which means "I will" plus the imperfective form and be understood. For that matter, you would be understood even if you used the perfective form with "Budu."

Once you know the "I" and "You" form, you simply drop the last letter of the "You" form to create the "He" and "She" form in the present.

For example: to call - volat. You call = Voláš, He calls = Volá or On volá, She calls = Ona volá

appear / zdát se (as in there appears to be an alien invasion) (not usually used with the "I" form)
you appear / zdáš se
zdál se (also used to say you dreamt) (see the verb Look)

ask / zeptat se/zeptám se, zeptáš se /
zeptal jsem se, zeptal se, zeptala se
ptát se ptám se, ptáš se
ptal se, Já jsem se ptal,

become
stát se/ stanu se, staneš se /
stal jsem se
stávat se - stávám se, stáváš se,
stával jsem se, On se stával, ona se stávala

begin
začít/začnu, začneš
začal
začínat / začínám, začínáš
začínal

believe
uvěřit / uvěřím, uvěříš
uvěřil
věřit / věřím, věříš
věřil jsem

bring / **přinést** / přinesu, přineseš
přinesl jsem, přinesl, přinesla
nést / nesu, neseš
nesl
(also, see wear)

buy / **koupit** / koupím, koupíš /
koupil jsem
kupovat / kupuju, kupuješ
kupoval jsem

call / **zavolat** /zavolám, zavoláš
zavolal, zavolala
volat / volám, voláš
volal jsem

cause / **způsobit**/způsobím, způsobíš
způsobil jsem
způsobovat /způsobuji, způsobuješ
způsoboval jsem

close / **zavřít** / zavřu, zavřeš /
zavřel jsem, zavřel, zavřela/
zavírat / zavírám, zavíráš
zavíral

come / **přijít** / přijdu, přijdeš /
přišel jsem, přišel, přišla
přicházet /přicházím, přicházíš
přicházel jsem

cook / **uvařit** / uvařím, uvaříš
uvařil jsem
vařit / vařím, vaříš
vařil

dance / **zatancovat si** / zatancuju si, zatancuješ si
zatancoval jsem si
tancovat/tancuji, tancuješ
tančil

decide / **rozhodnout se**/ rozhodnu se, rozhodneš se
rozhodl jsem se, rozhodl se, rozhodla se
rozhodovat se / rozhoduju se, rozhoduješ se
rozhodoval jsem se

drink / *napít se* / napiju se, napiješ se
napil jsem se
pít/ piju, piješ
pil jsem

drive / **řídit** / řídím, řídíš
řídil

*****do** / **udělat**-1/udělám, uděláš
udělal jsem
dělat / dělám, děláš
dělal jsem
*do and make are the same in Czech

eat / **sníst** / sním, sníš
snědl
jíst / jím, jíš
jedl jsem, jedl, jedla

end (v)**skončit** / skončím, skončíš /
l skončil, skončil, skončila
končit / končím, končíš
končil

to exit (get off) / **vystoupit** / vystoupím, vystoupíš/
vystoupil, on vystoupil, ona vystoupila
vystupovat / vystupuju, vystupovaš
vystupoval

exercise / **zacvičit si**/zacvičím si, zacvičíš se
zacvičil jsem si
cvičit/cvičím
cvičil jsem

exercise / **zacvičit si**/zacvičím si, zacvičíš se
zacvičil jsem si
cvičit/cvičím
cvičil jsem

feel / **cítit** / cítím, cítíš
cítila jsem, cítil, cítila

find / *najít* / najdu, najdeš
našel jsem, našel, našla

forget / **zapomenout** / zapomenu, zapomeneš
zapomněl jsem, zapomněl, ona zapomněla
zapomínat / zapomínám, zapomínáš
zapomínal

figure out / **vyřešit**/vyřeším, vyřešíš
vyřešil jsem
řešit / řeším, řešíš
řešil jsem

find out / **zjistit**/zjistím, zjistíš
zjistil jsem
zjišťovat / zjišťuji, zjišťuješ,
zjišťoval jsem

*get / **dostat** / dostanu, dostaneš
Dostal jsem, dostal, ona dostala
dostávat / dostávám, dostáváš
dostával
(*get has many meanings in English. It can mean obtain, receive, arrive, become among other meanings.)

get/become / stát se, stanu se, staneš se
stal jsem se
stávat se/stávám se, stáváš se
stával jsem se

get/arrive / přijet / přijedu, přijedeš
přijel jsem
přijíždět / přijíždím, přijíždíš
přijížděl jsem

give / dát /dám, dáš
dal jsem
dávat / dávám, dáváš
dával jsem

have / mít / mám, máš
měl jsem, měl, měla

have to-muset / musím, musíš
musel jsem

hear (v)slyšet / slyším, slyšíš
slyšel jsem

help / pomoct / pomohu, pomůžeš
pomohl, ona pomohla
pomáhat/pomáhám, pomáháš
pomáhal

hurry / spěchat / spěchám, spěcháš
spěchal jsem, spěchal, spěchala

keep (v)držet / držím, držíš
držel
podržet/podržím, podržíš
podržel

to kiss (v)políbit / políbím, políbíš
líbat / líbám, líbáš

know / vědět / vím, víš
věděl jsem

laugh / zasmát se / zasměju se, zasměješ se
zasmál se
smát se/směju se, směješ se
smál jsem se

learn / naučit se/naučím se, naučíš se
naučil jsem se
učit se / učím se, učíš se
učil jsem se

leave / nechat / nechám, necháš
nechal
nechávat / nechávám
nechával jsem

leave (depart) / odejít /odejdu, odejdeš
odešel jsem
odcházet / odcházím, odcházíš
odcházel jsem

to lie / zalhat / zalžu, zalžeš
zalhal
lhát / lžu, lžeš
lhal

like / mít rád (I like=mám rád)
mám rád, máš rád
měl jsem rad - I liked it.

listen / poslechnout si/poslechnu si, poslechneš si
poslechl jsem si
poslouchat/poslouchám, posloucháš
poslouchal jsem

love / milovat
miluju, miluješ
miloval

live / žít / žiju, žiješ
žil

look / podívat se / podívám se, podíváš se
podíval se
dívat se / dívám se, díváš se
díval se

look (as in seem or appear) **/ vypadat /** vypadám, vypadáš
vypadal
připadat si / připádam si, připadáš si
připadal si

look like / vypadat jako / vypadám jako, vypadáš, On vypadá jako

look for-hledat / hledám, hledáš
hledal jsem

make-do / udělat udělám, uděláš
udělal
dělat / dělám, děláš
dělal

need / potřebovat / potřebuju, potřebuješ
potřeboval jsem

order / objednat / objednám, objednáš
objednal
objednávat / objednávám, objednáváš
objednával

pay / zaplatit / zaplatím, zaplatíš
zaplatil
platit / platím, platíš
platil

plan / naplánovat / naplánuju, naplánuješ
naplánoval
plánovat / plánuju, plánuješ
plánoval

prepare / připravit / připravím, připravíš
připravil
připravovat / připravuju, připravuješ

to rain / pršet / prší
pršelo

realize / uvědomit si
uvědomím si, uvědomíš si
uvědomil si
uvědomovat si
uvědomuji si, uvědomuješ si
uvědomil (jsem) si

remember / zapamatovat si / zapamatuju si, zapamatuješ si
zapamatoval si
pamatovat si / pamatuju si, pamatuješ si
pamatoval si

repair / opravit/ opravím, opravíš
opravil
opravovat / opravuju, opravuješ
opravoval

return / vrátit 4 / vrátím, vrátíš
vrátil
vracet/ vracím, vracíš
vracel

save / ušetřit / ušetřím, ušetříš
ušetřil
šetřit / šetřím, šetříš
šetřil

say / říct řeknu, řekneš
řekl
říkat / říkám, říkáš
říkal

see / uvidět / uvidím, uvidíš
uviděl
vidět / vidím, vidíš
viděl

seem / (see the verb *look pg. 230*)

sell / prodat / prodám, prodáš/
prodal
prodávat / prodávám, prodáváš
prodával

send / poslat / pošlu, pošleš
poslal
posílat / posílám, posíláš
posílal

show / ukázat / ukážu, ukážeš
ukázal
ukazovat / ukazuju, ukazuješ
ukazoval

sit / sednout si / sednu si, sedneš si
sedl
sedět / sedím, sedíš
seděl

sleep / vyspat se / vyspím se, vyspíš se
vyspal se,
spat- spím, spíš
spal

speak / mluvit / mluvím, mluvíš
mluvil jsem

spend / utratit / utratím, utratíš
utratil
utrácet / utrácím, utrácíš
utrácel

start / začít / začnu, začneš
začal jsem, začal, začala
začínat / začínám, začínáš
začínal

stop / přestat / přestanu, přestaneš
přestal
přestávat / přestávám, přestáváš
přestával

study / nastudovat / nastuduju, nastuduješ
nastudoval
studovat /studuju, studuješ
studoval

suppose / předpokládat / předpokládám, předpokládáš
předpokládal

take / vzít / vezmu, vezmeš
vzal
brát / beru, bereš
bral

talk / promluvit / promluvím, promluvíš
promluvil
mluvit / mluvím, mluvíš
mluvil

teach / naučit / naučím, naučíš
naučil
učit / učím, učíš
učil

tell / říct řeknu, řekneš
řekl

thank / poděkovat / poděkuju, poděkuješ
poděkoval
děkovat / děkuju, děkuješ
děkoval

try / zkusit / zkusím, zkusíš
zkusil
zkoušet / zkouším, zkoušíš
zkoušel

understand / porozumět / porozumím, porozumíš
porozuměl
rozumět / rozumím, rozumíš
rozuměl

use / použít / použiju, použiješ
použil
používat / používám, používáš
používal

wait / počkat / počkám, počkáš
počkal
čekat / čekám, čekáš
čekal

walk projít se / projdu se, projdeš se
prošel se
procházet se / procházím se, procházíš se
procházel se

want / chtít / chci, chceš
chtěl

wash / umýt / umyju, umyješ
umyl
mýt / myju, myješ
myl

watch / podívat se / podívám se, podíváš se
podíval se
dívat se / dívám se, díváš se
díval se

wear / nosit / nosím, nosíš
nosil jsem

APPENDIX

work / pracovat / pracuju, pracuješ
pracoval

write / napsat / napíšu, napíšeš
napsal
psát / píšu, píšeš
psal

Of course, there are many exceptions. Two important irregluar verbs are:

"být" (to be): jsem, jsi, je, jsme, jste, jsou
"mít" (to have): mám, máš, má, máme, máte, mají

Other irregular verbs:

"chtít" (to want): chci, chceš, chce, chceme, chcete, chtějí
"vědět" (to know): vím, víš, ví, víme, víte, ví (or vědí)
"jíst" (to eat): jím, jíš, jí, jíme, jíte, jí (or jedí)
"spát" (to sleep): spím, spíš, spí, spíme, spíte, spí
"bát se" (to be afraid): bojím se, bojíš se, bojí se, bojíme se, bojíte se, bojí se
"stát" (to stand, to cost): stojím, stojíš, stojí, stojíme, stojíte, stojí
"stát se" (to happen, to become): stanu se, staneš se, stane se, staneme se, stanete se, stanou se
"číst" (to read): čtu, čteš, čte, čteme, čtete, čtou
"psát" (to write): píšu (or píši), píšeš, píše, píšeme, píšete, píšou (or píší)
"jít" (to go - walk): jdu, jdeš, jde, jdeme, jdete, jdou
"jet" (to go - drive or ride): jedu, jedeš, jede, jedeme, jedete, jedou
"vzít" (to take): vezmu, vezmeš, vezme, vezmeme, vezmete, vezmou
"růst" (to grow): rostu, rosteš, roste, rosteme, rostete, rostou

More Gender Grammar

When referring to *we* and *they,* formal Czech makes a distinction if the *we* and *they* are all men, all women, or a mixed gender group, or children. This distinction is not included in the Verb brain for čekat on page 39, where the default all male čekali form is used when the gender of the group is unknown. This distinction is not worth worrying about at this stage, as the pronunciation is the same and would be observed primarily in writing.

They waited: mixed gender: čekali
The men waited - čekali muži
The women waited - čekaly ženy
The children waited - čekaly děti

You could (plural)

Mixed group of men and women - mohli
All men - mohli
All women - mohly
(The pronunciation is the same)

You should (plural)

Mixed group of men and women - Měli
All men - Měli
All women - Měly
(The pronunciation is the same)

Alone - by myself

Czech uses the word *sám* to express the idea of being alone or doing something by oneself.

Sám

Are you alone? = Jsi sám?
Is he alone? = Je sám?
Is she alone? = Je to sama?
Are they alone? = Jsou sami?
Are we alone? = Jsme ve sami?

I am alone. = Jsem sám.
He is alone. = On je sám.
She is alone. = Ona je sama.
They are alone. = Jsou to sami.
We are alone. = Jsme sami.

I did it by myself. = Udělal jsem to sám.
You did it by yourself. = Udělal jsi to sám.
He did it by himself. = Udělal to sám.
she did it by herself. = Udělala to sám.
We did it by ourselves. = Udělali jsme to sámi.
You did it by yourselves. = Udělali jste to sámi.
They did it by themselves. = Udělali to sámi.

More on Money

Czech bill denominations:

One hundred crown note: Stovka
Two hundred crown note: Dvoustovka
Five hundred crown note: Pětistovka
Thousand crown note: Tisicovka
Two thousand crown note: Dvoutisicovka
Five thousand crown note: Pětisicovka

Czech coin denominations:

one crown coin - (jedna) koruna
two crown coin - dvoukoruna
five crown coin - pětikoruna
ten crown coin - desetikoruna
twenty crown coin - dvacetikoruna
fifty crown coin - padesátikoruna

But to say a number of individual coins:

one crown - jedna koruna
two crowns - dvě koruny
three crowns - tři koruny
four crowns - čtyři koruny

but from five crowns on up you use korun for the plural - pět korun

Abridged Dictionary
All Purpose Vocabulary

The useful words included here will allow you to talk about a variety of subjects in everyday life.

This short, all-purpose vocabulary list includes nouns about people, body, clothes, places, home, work transportation, money, culture, food, and nature.

Czech is a highly inflected language, that is words change in their appearance to show their grammatical role in the sentence. Before these changes can take place the words themselves must be categorized. In particular, nouns, verbs and adjectives require the following:

1. the classification of nouns into one of fourteen categories. see page 139.
2. the classification of verbs into one of four classes. see page 171.
3. the classification of adjectives into one of two categories. see page 165.

The words in this mini dictionary have been classified for your convenience.

Nouns - category shown by initials in parentheses ie., (mha), (mhi) and irregular plurals shown. (then refer to noun brain on page 139)
Verbs - first verb of pair is the perfective verb, the second, the imperfective. Some verbs have only one form in common usage.
Adjectives - the dictionary or nominative case of adjectives either end in ý or í.

ALL PURPOSE CZECH VOCABULARY

able (a)	schopný
afraid	obovát se
air (n)	vzduch (mhi)
angry (a)	rozzlobený
animal (n)	zviře (nme)
animals (n)	zvířata
anti-biotic (n)	antibiotika
anti-septic (n)	antiseptika
architecture (n)	architektura (fea)
arm (n)	paže (nme)
art (n)	umění (nei)
ask (v)	zeptat se / ptát se
aspirin (n)	aspirin (mhi)
baby (n)	miminko (neo)
back (n)	záda
backpack (n)	batoh (mhi)
bad	špatný
bag (n)	taška (fea)
ballet (n)	balet (mhi)
band aid (n)	leukoplast
bank (n)	banka (fea)
barber (n)	holičství
bathroom (n)	koupelna (fea)
bathtub (n)	vana (fea)
beach (n)	pláz (fs)
beautiful (a)	krásný
beauty (n)	krása (fea)
become (v)	stát se/ stávat se
bed (n)	postel (fee)
bedroom (n)	ložnice (fee)
begin (v)	začít /začínat
behind	za
believe (v)	uvěřit si / věřit si
bench (n)	lavička (fea)
best	nejlepší,
better	lepší,
big	velký
bird (n)	pták (mha)
birth (n)	narození (nei)

ALL PURPOSE CZECH VOCABULARY

black	černý

blanket (n)	deka (fea)
blood (n)	krev (fs)
blue	modrý
body (n)	tělo (neo)
book (n)	kniha (fea)
bookcase (n)	knihovna (fea)
bookstore (n)	knihkupectvi (nei)
bowls (n)	miska
boy (n)	kluk (mha)
boys (n)	kluci
brain (n)	mozek (mhi)
breasts (n)	prso-a (neo)
bridge (n)	most (mhi)
bring (v)	přinést si-/ nést
broken	zlomený
brother (n)	bratr (mha)
buildings (n)	budova (fea)
burners (on stove) (n)	plotna (fea)
bus stop (n)	autobusová stanice
bush (n)	křoví (nea)
busy	zaměstnaný
butt (n)	zadek (mhi) or predélka (fea)
buy (v)	koupit / kupovat
call (v)	zavolat / volat
calm	klidný
carpet (n)	koberec (msi)
cassette (n)	kazeta (fea)
cat (n)	kočka (fea)
cd player (n)	cédečko (neo)
ceiling (n)	(strop)
chair (n)	zidle (fee)
cheap	levný
child (n)	dítě (nme)
children (n)	děti
church (n)	kostel (mhi)
cinema (n)	kino (neo)
city (n)	velkoměsto (neo)
classics (n)	klasická
classroom (n)	třída (fea)

ALL PURPOSE CZECH VOCABULARY

clean	čistý
clock (n)	hodiny
close (v)	zavřít /zavírat
closet (n)	skřiň (fee)
cloud (n)	mrak (mhi)
coat (n)	bunda (fea)
coffee table (n)	konfernční stolek
cold	studený
college (n)	vysoká škola
come (v)	přijít / přicházet
communication	komunikace (fee)
company (n)	splolečnost (fh)
complex	úplný
computer (n)	počitač
concert (n)	koncert (mhi)
continue (v)	pokračovat (v)
cook (v)	uvařit si /vařit si
cost (v)	stát (1)
counter top (n)	deska
country (n)	příroda (fea)
court (n)	dvůr
crazy	bláznivý
culture (n)	kultura (fea)
cupboards (n)	linka (fea)
curtain (n)	zaclona (fea)
dad (n)	táta
dance (v)	zatancovat/tancovat
dance	tanec (msi)
dark	tmavý
death (n)	smrt (fhi)
decide (v)	rozhodnout se
delicious	výborný
dentist's office (n)	zubaří
depressed	depresi
desk (n)	psaci stůl (mhi)
dictionary (n)	slovník (mi)
difficult	složitý
dirt/soil (n)	hlína (fea)
dirty	špinavý

ALL PURPOSE CZECH VOCABULARY

disco (n)	diskotéka (fea)
district (n)	čtvrtě
doctor's office (n)	doktoroví
dog (n)	pes (mha)
door (n)	dveře
drawer (n)	šuplík (mhi)
dream (n)	zdát se (snit
dress (n)	šaty
dresser (n)	stolek (mhi)
drink (v)	napít se
drink (n)	pití/ nápoj
drive (v)	řídit
dry	suchý
ear(s) (n)	ucho,uši (neo)
earth (n)	země (fee)
easy	lehký-snadný
eat (v)	sníst / jíst
education (n)	vzdělání
electric	elektrický
end (v)	skončit / končit
enjoy (v)	líbit se
enter (v)	vstoupit / vstupovat
environment (n)	prostředí (nea)
event (n)	akce
example (n)	přiklad (mhi)
excellent	vyborný
to exit, (v)	vystoupit / vystupovat
the exit (n),	východ
expensive	drahý
eye(s) (n)	oko-oči (neo)
fantastic	fantastický
farm (n)	farma (fea)
fast	rychlý
fat	tlustý
father (n)	otec (msa)
faucet (n)	kohoutek (mhi)
feel (v)	cítit-3
foot, feet (n)	chodidlo-a (neo)
female (n)	žena (fea)
film (n)	film (mhi)

ALL PURPOSE CZECH VOCABULARY

find (v)	najít
fingers (n)	prst-prsty (mhi)
to finish	končit
fire (n)	ohně (msi)
fireman (n)	hasič
fish (n)	ryba (fea)
fitness center (n)	fitness centrum
flat (n)	byt (mhi)
floor (n)	podlaha
florist (n)	květinářstvi (nei)
flower (n)	květina (fea)
forest (n)	les (mhi)
forget (v)	zapomenout / zapomínat
fork (n)	vidlička (fea)
freezer (n)	mrazák (mhi)
fresh	čerstvý
friendly	přátelský
funny	legrační,
garage (n)	same (fee)
garden (n)	zahrada (fea)
gas station (n)	čerpací stanice (fee)
gas (n)	plyn (mhi)
get (v)	dostat-/dostávat
girl (n)	holka (fea)
give (v)	dát-/ dávat-
glass (n)	sklenička (fea)
go (v)	jít (L-form:šel)/ chodit
good	dobrý dobrá dobré
grass (n)	tráva (fea)
great	veliký,skvělý
green	zelený
ground (n)	země (fee)
hairdresser (n)	kadeřnictví (nei)
hallway (n)	chodba (fea)
hand(s) (n)	ruka,ruce (fea)
happy	štastný, veselý
hard	tvrdý
have (v)	mít
head (n)	hlava (fea)

ALL PURPOSE CZECH VOCABULARY

hear (v)	slyšet
heart (n)	srdce (nee)
heavy	těžký
help (v)	pomoct / pomáhat
history (n)	historie (fee)
home (n)	domov (mhi)
hope	doufat
hospital (n)	nemocnice (fee)
hot	horký
house (n)	dům (mhi)
hungry	hladový
hurry (v)	spěchat
husband (n)	manžel (mha)
important	důležitý
insect (n)	hmyz (mhi)
jacket (n)	kabát (mhi)
keep (v)	držet / podržet
to kiss (v)	políbit / libat
a kiss	polibek
kitchen (n)	kuchyně (fee)
knife (n)	nůz (msi)
knobs (n)	klika (fea)
know (v)	vědět
lake (n)	jezero (neo)
laugh (v)	zasmát se / smát se
law (n)	zákon (mha)
lawyer (n)	právník (mha)
learn (v)	naučit se / učit se
leave (v)	nechat / nechávat
legs (n)	noha-nohy (fea)
library (n)	knihovna (fea)
a lie	lež
to lie (v)	zalhat / lhát
light bulb (n)	žárovka (fea)
light (weight)	lehký
light (n)	světlo (neo)
light	světlý
light switch (n)	vypinač (msi)
like (v)	mít rád (I like=mám rád)
lip(s) (n)	ret, rty (mhi)

listen (v)	poslouchat
literature (n)	literatura (fea)
live (v)	žít
lizard (n)	ještěr (mha)
long	dlouhý
look (v)	podívat / dívat
look for	hledat si
loud	hlasitý
love (v)	milovat
lucky	štastný
magazine (n)	časopis (mhi)
make-do (v)	udělat /dělat
male (n)	muž (msa)
man	muž
mathematics (n)	matematika (fea)
medicine (n)	medicina (fea)
meet	potkát /potkávat
men (n)	muži (msa)
military (n)	armáda (fea)
the mind (n)	misl
miss (n)	slečna (fea)
mobile phones (n)	mobílní telefon (mhi)
mom (n)	máma
moon (n)	měsíce (mse)
mother (n)	matka (fea)
mountain (n)	hora (fea)
Mr.	pán
Mrs.	paní
mud (n)	bláto (neo)
music (n)	hudba (fea)
musicians (n)	hudebník (mha)
must	muset
napkin (n)	ubrousek (mhi)
nation (n)	narod (mhi)
neat	přijemný
necessary	nezbytný
need (v)	potřebovat
nervous	nervový
new	nový
newspaper (n)	noviny

nice	pěkný
night club (n)	noční podnik (mhi)
nose	nos (mhi)
ocean (n)	oceán (mhi)
office (n)	kancelař (fs)
office (n)	úřad (mhi)
old	starý
open	otevřít si / otevírat si
opera (n)	opera
orchestra (n)	symfonický (mhi)
order (v)	objednat / objednávat
outside	venku
oven	trouba (fea)
pants (n)	kalhoty
paper (n)	papír (mhi)
park (n)	park (mhi)
party (n)	oslava (fea)
pay (v)	zaplatit / platit
peace (n)	mír
pen (n)	pero (neo)
pencil (n)	tužka (fea)
penis (n)	penis
people (n)	lidi (mhi)
person (n)	člověk (mha)
pharmacy (n)	lékárná (fea)
philosophy (n)	filosofie (fee)
picture (n)	obraz (mhi)
pillow (n)	polštář
plan (v)	naplánovat / plánovat
planet (n)	planeta (fea)
plant (n)	rostlina (fea)
plate/s (n)	talíř/e
play	zahrát / hrát
police station (n)	policejní úřad
police (n)	policie (fee)
politics (n)	politika (fea)
post office (n)	pošta (fea)
prepare (v)	připravit / připravovat
pronunciation (n)	výslovnost
psychology (n)	psychologie (fee)
pub/bar (n)	hospoda (fea)

ALL PURPOSE CZECH VOCABULARY

purse (n)	kabelka (fea)
put	položit
quiet	tichý
radio (n)	rádio
rain (n)	deště (mse)
to rain (v)	pršet
read	přečíst si / číst si
ready	připravený
realize (v)	uvědomit si
reception (n)	recepce (fee)
red	černý
refrigerator (n)	lednička (fea)
relaxed	uvolněný
religion (n)	nábozenství (nei)
remember (v)	zapamatovat si / pamatovat si
repair (v)	opravit / opravovat
reptile (n)	plaz (mha)
resource (n)	zdroj (mse)
restaurant (n)	restaurace (fee)
return (v)	vrátit 4 / vracet
river (n)	řeka (fea)
rock (n)	skála (fea)
rotten	shnilý
rough	hrubý
rug (n)	koberec (msi)
sad	smutný
salty	slaný
sand (n)	písek (mhi)
save (v)	ušetřit / šetřit
say (v)	řict si / řikat si
school (n)	škola (fea)
science (n)	věda (fea)
sea (n)	moře (nee)
search (v)	najít si / hledat si
see (v)	uvidět (4)/vidět (4)
seem (v)	zdát se
sell (v)	prodat / prodávat
send (v)	poslat
sheets (n)	desky
shelf (n)	polička (fea)

shoe (n)	bota (fea)
shopping center (n)	obchodní středisko
short	krátký
show (v)	ukázat /ukazovat
simple	snadný, jednoduchy
sink	umyvadlo (neo)
sister	sestra (fea)
sit (v)	sednout si /sedět
skin (n)	kuže (fee)
sky (n)	nebe (nee)
sleep (v)	spát
slow	pomalý
small town (n)	městečko (neo)
small	malý
smoke (n)	kouř (msi)
smooth	hladký
snake (n)	had (mha)
snow (n)	sníh (mhi)
socks (n)	ponožka (fea)
sofa (n)	pohovka (fea)
soft	měkký
speak (v)	mluvit si (4)
spend (v)	utratit / utrácet
spicy	pálivý, ostrý
spoiled	rozlmazlený
sponge (n)	Mycí houba
spoon (n)	lžička (fea)
square	náměstí (nei)
square	čtverec
stapler (n)	sešívačka (fea)
star (n)	hvězda (fea)
start (v)	začít / začínat
stay	zůstat / zůstávat
stone (n)	kámen (msi)
stop (v)	přestat / přestávat
store (n)	obchod (mhi)
stove (n)	sporak (mhi)
stream (n)	potok (mhi)

ALL PURPOSE CZECH VOCABULARY

street (n)	ulice (fee)
study (v)	nastudovat / studovat
subject (n)	předmět (mhi)
suburbs (n)	předměstí (nei)
Sun (n)	slunce (nee)
supermarket (n)	supermarket
suppose (v)	předpokládat
sweet	sladký
swimming pool (n)	bazén (mhi)
table (n)	stůl
take (v)	vzít si / brat si
talk (v)	promluvit / mluvit
tall	dlouhý, vysoký
tape player (n)	kazeták (mhi)
teach (v)	naučit se / učit se
telephone (n)	telefon (mhi)
tell (v)	řict si / řikat si
temperature (n)	teplota (fea)
tennis courts (n)	kurt (mhi)
terrible	hrozný
thank (v)	poděkovat / děkovat
theater (n)	divadlo (neo)
thick	tlustý
thin	tenký
think (v)	vymyslet si / myslet si
thirsty	žíznivý
tired	unavený
toaster (n)	opékač
toilet (n)	toaleta (fea)
tongue (n)	jazyk (mhi)
tools (n)	nářadí (nei)
towels (n)	ručnik (nei)
town (n)	město
tram (n)	stoop tramvajová zastávka
tree (n)	strom (mhi)
truth (n)	pravda (fea)
try (v)	zkusit / zkoušet
t-shirt (n)	tryčko (neo)
TV (n)	televize (fee)
ugly	ošklivý

ALL PURPOSE CZECH VOCABULARY

understand (v)	porozumět / rozumět

use (v)	použít / používat
vagina (n)	vagina (fea)
village (n)	vesnice (fee)
wait (v)	počkat / čekat
walk (v)	projít se / procházet se
wall (n)	zeď (fh)
wallet (n)	peněženka (fea)
want (v)	chtít
war (n)	valka (fea)
warm	teplý
wash cloth (n)	uěrka (fea)
wash (v)	umýt / mýt
washing machine (n)	myčka nádobí (fea)
watch (n)	hodinky
watch (v)	podívat se / dívat se
wear (v)	nosit
weather (n)	počasi (nei)
wet	mokrý
white	bílý
wife (n)	manželka (fea)
wind (n)	větry (mhi)
window (n)	okno (neo)
to wish (v)	přát
a wish (n)	přání
woman (n)	žena (fea)
woman	ženou (instrumental case)
women (n)	ženy (plural)
woods (n)	venkov (mhi)
work (v)	pracovat
write (v)	napsat si / psát si

251

About the Author

William G. Karneges, M.Sc.candidate, is an innovator, teacher and author of books on language, chess and memory. In Speak Czech Badly, he shares his "Language Brain" innovation and offers insight into the workings of the labyrinth of the Czech language. He's proud to say he speaks Czech badly.

www.ingramcontent.com/pod-product-compliance
Lightning Source LLC
Chambersburg PA
CBHW071707160426
43195CB00012B/1610